Teenage

Suicide

Teenage Suicide

Sandra Gardner
with Gary B. Rosenberg, M.D.

REVISED EDITION

JULIAN ⊗ MESSNER

Published by Julian Messner, a division of
Silver Burdett Press, Inc., Simon & Schuster, Inc.
Prentice Hall Bldg., Englewood Cliffs, NJ 07632.

JULIAN MESSNER and colophon are trademarks
of Simon & Schuster, Inc.
Design by Malle N. Whitaker

Manufactured in the United States of America.
The excerpt from *Dead Poets Society* on p. 78 is copyright
© Touchstone Films and used with their permission.

Lib. ed.   10   9   8   7   6   5   4   3   2   1
Paper ed. 10   9   8   7   6   5   4   3   2   1

Library of Congress Cataloging-in-Publication Data

Gardner, Sandra.
    Teenage suicide/Sandra Gardner with Gary B.
Rosenberg . — rev. ed.
        p. cm
    Includes bibliographical references.
    Summary: Examines some of the reasons and causes for
teenage suicide and other self-destructive behavior and
discusses what can be done about this increasing problem.
        1. Teenagers—United States—Suicidal behavior—Case
studies—Juvenile literature.   2. Adolescent psychology—
Juvenile literature.   3. Suicide—United States—Prevention—
Juvenile literature.   4. Puberty—Juvenile literature.   [1.
Suicide.]
    I. Rosenberg, Gary B.   II. Title.
    HV6546.G37 1990
    362.2'8'0835—dc20   89-49586
    ISBN 0-671-70200-9   ISBN 0-671-70201-7 (pbk.)   CIP
                                                          AC

Acknowledgments

To Fair Oaks Hospital and to Katharine Lindner, Chief Librarian of the Englewood Hospital Medical Library, for valuable assistance—and to my husband, Lewis Gardner, for his patience and understanding.

S.G.

I would like to thank my wife, Dara Justine Rosenberg, who contributed to the editing.

G.B.R.

Contents

Teenage

Suicide

Introduction

Growing up can be easy. Growing up can be hard. Where am I going? Who am I? Who do I want to be? When you enter adolescence, views of yourself and others change. The physical changes of puberty create an entirely different body and mind. The body transforms into a different size and shape. The mind experiences new feelings and thoughts. Parents, friends, teachers, coaches, and siblings begin to assume different attitudes and roles. People expect you to behave like an adult yet often continue to treat you like a child.

As an adolescent, you expect people to treat you differently. Prior to adolescence, you are faced with the need to establish trust in others, sense of self, a secure place in the family, and positive relationships with peers and adults in the community. During adolescence all of these tasks need to be confronted and resolved again.

The entire process of puberty and adolescence can be happy or sad, satisfying or frustrating, hopeful or futile. Despite it all, most adolescents will experience problems that they will be able to resolve. However, some poeple will experience significant problems. Although some problems will be resolved, others will not.

Suicide can be the unfortunate answer for some to the futility, sadness, and frustration of adolescence. Suicide has become the solution for more and more adolescents during the last several years. For a variety of reasons, it has become increasingly difficult to be an adolescent. Cultural, social, biological, and psychological forces can join to create what is felt to be unbearable stress.

The fact that the incidence of suicide is a culture-related phenomenon is demonstrated by the different rates of suicide in different countries. In general, higher rates of suicide are found in Western societies than in Eastern. Social factors interplay with these cultural determinants. There is speculation that the recent increase in such social phenomena as divorce, political turmoil, family mobility, and maternal employment have created an environment ripe for childhood and adolescent emotional upheaval.

Adolescents are confronted with the need to accomplish the resolution of important psychological tasks. This includes the establishment of an independent identity and an ability to relate to others in an intimate fashion. The ability to resolve these tasks is clearly related to the adolescent's family life experience. Cultural determinants, social upheaval, and psychological distress may join together to create emotional difficulties. If someone is biologically predestined to experience depression or to be intolerant of frustration and coincidentally has thought of suicide as a response to stress, then emotional difficulties may catalyze suicidal behavior.

Suicidal behavior is the response of some to emotional distress. It need not be the response for anyone. Stress can be responded to in a more appropriate and effective way. If suicide is your only option, then you are not allowing yourself to see all the other options that exist. It is often necessary to communicate your problems to a parent, a friend, a teacher, a coach, or a therapist. If you can *listen*, then you will *hear* all the other options that exist to resolve stress. All that remains will be the need to take a risk—a risk to confront and resolve your problems, and to expose your fears and concerns. The ability to talk openly and honestly about worries and problems will create the opening of choices and alternatives that don't exist when you remain closed, fearful, and frustrated.

A suicidal person has trapped himself or herself in a corner. The escape from that trap is possible when the suicidal person can take a risk and view the dilemma from a new perspective and be open to establishing new ideas and behaviors.

Gary B. Rosenberg, M.D.

Teenage
Suicide

CHAPTER ONE

Six Who

Tried

to Die

Patty, Johnny, Debbie, Marilyn, Lauren, and Carl are all young people from middle-class families. They have something else in common too: each has tried to commit suicide.

Fifteen minutes after a math teacher told Patty she was failing for the semester, Patty went to her gym locker, took out a bottle of Tylenol, and swallowed half the contents—about thirty pills. Woozy, feeling more and more faint, she sat through two more classes before her fear of dying overcame her desire to die and she told a teacher.

"When I heard about the failure for the marking period, that broke the camel's back," says fifteen-year-old Patty.

For Patty, "the straw that broke the camel's back," as she put it, was the math teacher's confronting her with the failing grade. This was the latest in a long list of what she considered failures—in school, at home, with peers.

There were many problems that led up to that fateful day in May. Not only was Patty doing poorly in math, but because of an undiagnosed learning disability, she had trouble with schoolwork in general.

Patty had learning disabilities that were unrecognized for years, not only by her parents, but by her teachers as well. Patty tried to master her subject matter, only to fail constantly and fall further and further behind. All the while, the adults around her were criticizing her for not "doing her best." Patty faced impossible tasks in school in trying to keep up with her parents', teachers', and her own expectations. She grew more and more depressed. Not wanting to be a troublemaker in school, she was quiet about her distress, so no one knew how she felt.

Patty also had difficulty making friends and was teased or ignored by her classmates. She felt isolated and alienated around other young people.

In addition, she had trouble with her family. Her mother had had twin babies a year before and they took a lot of her attention and time. Patty resented them and her popular, smart, thirteen-year-old sister, Gloria. But at home, too, Patty kept her feelings to herself. Her problems gradually grew into a mountain of despair, and she felt she had no way out.

"I just couldn't take it anymore," she says.

When Patty's mother received the news from school about Patty's suicide attempt, she didn't believe it.

"Patty is prone to exaggeration, prone to lying, so I thought that this was another thing she did to get attention. I was in total disbelief."

Patty's mother got to the school an hour later. Before taking Patty to the emergency room, she brought Patty home so that she could drop off the twins with Gloria.

"Gloria was very angry at Patty when all this happened," says Patty's mother. "When I told her what Patty had done, she was screaming at her, saying, 'How could you do something like that?'"

Patty stood there, silent, with the poison still in her system. Finally, mother and daughter arrived at the local emergency room.

"After they did some blood workup, they told me she'd taken a minimum of twenty to twenty-five pills," her mother says. "I was shocked that Patty would do something so drastic just to get my undivided attention."

Patty's need to get her mother's attention away from the demanding twins and her sister, Gloria, had nearly killed her.

Fifteen-year-old Johnny had been acting out—getting in trouble at home, in school, and with the law. He and his friends would hang around drinking and smoking pot. Sometimes they'd mug someone and steal a purse.

"They never even needed the money," says Johnny about his friends. "They just did it for the excitement."

When Johnny was in seventh grade, his parents separated for the second time. That year he didn't do much in school and had to repeat the grade. He tried to kill himself when he'd just turned thirteen. That afternoon, he recalls, he'd had a big argument in school with one of his teachers.

"I just stormed out of the room and slammed the door, and the glass shattered. And then I just walked right out of the school and went home and took the pills. I took a whole bottle of buffered aspirin, and I lay down and went to sleep. When I woke up, I didn't even have a stomach ache."

No one knew about Johnny's suicide attempt until after his second try, when he was fifteen. He gulped down another bottle of pills while his parents were sleeping in the next room.

"I don't know why I did it," he says about his second attempt. "I just wanted to go to sleep and not wake up.

Because I couldn't care less about anything that happens now. Like I don't get mad. I don't get extremely happy. I just don't let anything affect me."

Even when he talks about his girlfriend of two years whom he broke up with two weeks before he downed the bottle of pills, he shrugs, claiming she really didn't matter to him.

"We just started bickering all the time, and I didn't need the aggravation," he recounts. "We'd argue about the littlest things, from what TV stations to watch to where she had been the night before."

Johnny's relationship with his family was virtually nonexistent at that point. Even now, though he is getting help, he has a great deal of trouble relating.

"I have a finished room in the basement. I just walk in the back door whenever I want and go right downstairs. I don't have to be bothered with any of them."

Although Johnny doesn't realize it, he is really terribly affected by how other people react to him. If he feels ignored or not taken seriously, he can get depressed or even violent.

It happened one day at the hospital where Johnny was getting help.

"One of the mental health workers said I wasn't allowed to go outside, for my own protection," he said. "I said to her that it was much easier to hurt myself inside than outside. And she, like, blanked me out. So I pushed her out of the way and banged the window again and again with my forehead until the window broke."

With his peers, Johnny's sensitivity to being ignored can overpower him.

"One girl at the hospital wanted my advice, so I started to give it, and she interrupted me when I was speaking. She said, 'Oh, you don't understand. Maybe I should go talk to someone else.' I said, 'Fine,' and just stood up and walked to my room. And I started getting down. I don't even know why."

On another occasion, Johnny says, "I almost beat up one of the kids at a group therapy meeting—because he interrupted me."

And if Johnny finally dares to make his feelings known, and he isn't taken seriously, it can catapult him toward danger.

"If I say I feel like jumping out a window, and someone says, 'Oh, come on, don't be ridiculous,' that will push me to do it all the more," he says.

Johnny's defense is to tune people—and his own feelings—out. He does this to keep painful things from getting to him, such as the constant fighting between his parents, his father's aloofness, the beatings Johnny got when he was younger. Although his brothers were also beaten, they were able to express their anger.

Not so Johnny.

"When I was little, I used to get hit with a leather belt around my neck, in front of all my friends. My father did that when I was in the fifth grade. But I just laughed. It didn't matter," he shrugs.

Both parents often worked long hours when Johnny was younger, and he was left alone a lot. This, too, he says, didn't matter.

"I like to be alone," he claims.

Nothing got to Johnny—or so he says. But on a Sunday night in June, he went into his bathroom and swallowed a bottle of pills.

He had fantasies about the reactions to his funeral.

"Like, my friends, they would say, like, 'Wow, Johnny did that.' I'd have them puzzled," he says.

Even in talking about his suicide attempt, Johnny couldn't acknowledge that it was his parents whose emotional reaction he'd longed for.

The "trigger" for Johnny's suicide attempt was a seemingly trivial event—breaking up with a girlfriend who, he asserted, didn't even mean very much to him. But whether Johnny, who tuned the world out and turned himself off, could even admit to himself that she did matter is still a question.

Thirteen-year-old Debbie began "feeling numb" one winter.

"Like I wasn't real, I wasn't alive. I was always crying and I didn't know why."

Every night for a month, Debbie cut skin off her wrists with a razor blade. The only way she knew she was real, she says, was when she saw the blood.

"I couldn't stop. I'd be on the phone with my friends, having a good conversation. And all of a sudden, there was all this blood pouring out of my wrists."

Debbie is very close to her fifteen-year-old brother.

"He reminded me of things that happened that I didn't remember."

These events were the battles her divorced parents had over her the summer before. She'd been spending time visiting her father and stepmother at their summer place, where she had met a new boyfriend.

"After I'd speak to my mother on the phone, I'd throw up. I'd get physically sick because I didn't want to go back home. I hated her.

"My mother didn't like me," says Debbie. "I'd come home from school and we'd fight about everything. My friends would come over and my mom would make them leave and yell at me. She'd say, 'Your friends can't stay, they've got to go home.' And I'd have to go to my room. But it was nothing against my friends, it was against me. She didn't like me."

Debbie also felt she was being pulled back and forth between her parents. This feeling had existed for years, but the summer before her suicide attempts, it came to a head when she stayed with her father and felt disloyal to her mother. Debbie says that she "didn't even remember" all the phone calls from her mother that upset her so until her brother reminded her long afterward. The following winter Debbie blocked out all her feelings and couldn't feel "real."

Debbie was questioned about her loyalty by one parent when she wanted to be with the other.

"Family problems were there all my life," she says. "I was caught in the middle of the divorce. I was getting pressure on both ends. My dad wanted to get back at my mom, and he tried to use me to do it. They put me in the middle a lot. It was awful."

Although she still doesn't feel real sometimes, she says she's better off than one of her friends, who also tried to kill herself.

"Her dad died and she was abused by her mom. Her mom kicked her out. She slit her wrists and her mom still wouldn't give her help. Finally, she OD'd. She's in the hospital now."

Debbie, caught in the middle of her parents' divorce, seems to have a special sensitivity to pain—her own and others'—that caused her to feel so depressed.

"It was awful," she repeated over and over again, about her parents' fighting. About the way she felt pulled between them. About not wanting to hurt either of them with her "disloyalty." About her friend's situation and the pain she experienced for her.

Luckily Debbie has been learning to deal with her feelings. Although she may always be a sensitive person, being able to express her feelings has helped her to become stronger and better able to cope with problems. Before she learned to do that, her emotions overwhelmed her so that she "became numb" and felt the only way out was suicide.

Sometimes a brother or sister can help a troubled person. But sometimes that person can make the situation worse.

When fourteen-year-old Marilyn was small, her best friend was her sister, Nancy, who was ten years older. But when Marilyn was seven, Nancy got pregnant and got married and moved out. That's when Marilyn's problems began. She felt her sister had abandoned her.

Their mother had let Nancy take care of Marilyn a lot when she was younger.

"We were always together," Marilyn recalls. "She took me everywhere."

When Marilyn was nine, Nancy, divorced, moved back home with her child. However, instead of having her sister's attention again, Marilyn found that the family's attention was now focused on the baby.

"I didn't like my sister's son at all," says Marilyn, "because he took her away from me. To this day, it's still a problem. But my parents expected me to be nice to him because of the way Nancy was to me."

Even after Nancy moved away again, Marilyn still felt ignored. Her parents were constantly fighting and were considering divorce.

"They asked me to decide which one I would live with. I couldn't really handle that. I told them that I couldn't make that decision."

Marilyn says, "My family rejected me. I used to do pretty good in school. But no matter what I did, it wasn't good enough. No matter what, it didn't please them. They used to say nasty things about me screwing up. They didn't realize that it hurt me."

Marilyn's sister had rebelled against their straight-laced parents by becoming pregnant. Marilyn paid for that rebellion in her small town by getting a "bad reputation" among her peers.

"She was called a whore and a slut," Marilyn's mother says. "It wouldn't stop."

Alienated from her family and her classmates, Marilyn chose alcohol and drugs as a way out of her anger and pain. Some psychiatrists and psychologists call the process of easing pain with drugs and alcohol "self-medication."

Marilyn turned to drink when she was eleven years old.

"I've always hung out with people older than me," she says. "We'd find somebody to get us beers and just go to the park and drink. It wasn't until I was thirteen that I got into acid and mescaline and dust and things like that. I cut classes every day. All day, I'd just sit and drink and smoke pot."

When she was fourteen, she took mescaline and drank with some friends one night in an abandoned house. She ended up trying to kill herself and another girl with a razor blade, besides nearly dying from convulsions.

"I was very, very foggy and out of it," she says of that night.

After calling everywhere, her parents finally found her and took her home.

Marilyn had tried to die once before. Like Johnny, she hadn't told anyone.

"When I was in the sixth grade, I took a lot of Percodans, some kind of tranquilizer my mother had at home. I was crying a lot, and the next day I was pretty out of it. They didn't find out about it until a year later, because my mother hardly ever used those pills."

Marilyn's father remarks, "I think kids are awfully good at fooling their parents into thinking there's nothing wrong." He admits that between working, helping the older kids in school, and the comings and goings of Nancy and her baby, he "kind of ignored" Marilyn.

Marilyn sees her family relationships as her main problem. "My family had nothing to do with me. My mother wouldn't talk to me. She yelled at me and she put me down for everything. My parents said they didn't know I was doing drugs. But, really, I think they were just denying it. I had a terrible relationship with my parents."

When Lauren, now seventeen, was in the fifth grade, she began worrying about her weight. Even more than that, her physical development scared her and was the source of embarrassment and teasing by the boys she played baseball with.

Lauren says she was a "tomboy" when she was a little girl.

"I played a lot of football and baseball," she comments.

That part of her childhood was a happy one, she recalls. It was a period when she and her father and brother spent time together.

"But then I got my period in the fifth grade. And the older guys we played ball with noticed I was developing and made comments. I felt really self-conscious and upset. When I stopped eating in the sixth grade, I stopped getting my period. And I was very happy about that."

Lauren equated her budding womanhood in the fifth grade with a sense of loss. It was the end of a playful companionship with her father and brother. She became fearful of growing up sexually. Even now, at seventeen, she admits that she's leery of the idea of a sexual relationship.

Lauren disliked herself and her body. When she would get very depressed, she would binge on food and then she'd vomit. Or she'd fast for a couple of days and then binge and throw up again. This binge/purge syndrome is called bulimia. It affects many young women and occasionally young men.

Besides her fear of growing up, Lauren, always a good student, developed a fear of school that lasted through high school. Lauren's school phobia, which, like bulimia, is a diagnosable, treatable, psychological problem, built up for years, until she felt having to go to school was "death."

School phobics feel intense anxiety that is connected with a fear of failure and the setting of unrealistic goals by themselves, their parents, and their school. Rather than take a chance on herself in class, where she might not be "perfect," Lauren felt she would rather die.

"I always felt inadequate," she remembers.

Why did Lauren want to end her life?

"Nobody cared," she says. "The only time I ever saw my father show emotion was when a doctor told him I had tried to kill myself. And my mother and I were always fighting. I didn't think anybody really wanted me. I didn't get along with my parents at all."

Lauren also felt hopeless about her future.

"I didn't think anything would get better. I didn't think I could ever go to school. I was afraid of everyone, especially people my own age and especially guys. I couldn't understand why I was feeling so bad. There was so much pain. And I always felt people were going to leave me."

Just before Lauren was supposed to enter eighth grade, she took sulfa drugs and a number of other prescription medications and nearly died.

"I was pretty sick the next day," she recalls. "But gradually, after a while, I wasn't afraid to do it anymore. I always thought, maybe if I'm lucky, I'll die."

When the next year's deadline for school came around, Lauren decided she wasn't going to leave dying to chance.

"I figured, 'Well, you took all those pills that time you didn't want to go to school; you might as well not live until next year.' It was New Year's Eve. That's when I did it."

Lauren was fourteen then. Everyone was out of the house except her younger brother and his friend, who were watching TV.

"I took even more pills this time. And I took my mother's vodka, put some orange juice in it, and shook it up. I drank it all in the shower.

"God, the room was spinning. I came out and thought I was just going to lie down on the bed. I had this great fantasy: to lie down in bed, go to sleep, and just never wake up again."

Lauren's mother recalls, "Lauren had it very difficult from the day she was born. She was born into a family where my mother was crying all the time. Then, later, my mother-in-law was crying."

When she was pregnant with Lauren, her father died. Then, when Lauren was three, Lauren's other grandfather died. When she was four, her parents first separated, and her father left the house.

"And," says her mother, "when Lauren was eight, my grandfather died. The men in her life all walked away from her."

Carl's father shot himself in Carl's bathroom when Carl was fifteen.

Carl has a brother two years younger. Their parents divorced when Carl was eight. His father lived nearby for a while and there were frequent visits. But when Carl was fourteen, his father moved to the South.

Carl, who had always idolized his father, joined him during the summer with plans to live with him permanently. His father was busy trying to make a new start. He tried to set up a business, failed, and became more and more depressed.

His mother's and father's families lived nearby in the same southern state. Eight months after Carl moved in, his father picked him up from baseball practice and dropped him off at his grandmother's for their usual Friday night family dinner. Two months before, Carl's father had bought a .357 magnum gun.

"He said it was for target practice and I believed him," Carl says. "My uncle has about thirty guns."

About forty-five minutes after Carl arrived at his grandmother's, the police called and told the family that Carl's father had shot himself in the head.

"I just went bozo," Carl recalls. "I hit the wall, bloodied my hands and stuff. I was angry at him for doing this. But," he adds quickly, "he really didn't do it to hurt anybody. He just did it so he wouldn't be depressed. And that's how it was when I attempted suicide."

Carl was not really able to let himself get angry at his father for committing suicide. However, his younger brother, Billy, was able to yell and scream at their mother about his anger at their father's suicide.

Their mother recalls, "Three weeks after the suicide, Billy cried, came into my room, picked something up and threw it across the room, saying, 'I hate my father. How could he do this to me?' He got it out," she says. "Carl can't get it out."

Carl had suffered a symbolic loss of his father for years, ever since his parents divorced. He suffered again when his father moved away. The final, irrevocable loss occurred when Carl's father killed himself. Carl had to bear his unadmitted anger at his father's abandonment as well as his own sense of guilt. Often, when someone dies, those close to that person feel a "survivor's guilt," a sense of guilt for being alive while that other person is dead.

Carl says, "I just didn't know my father as well as I thought I did. If I had, I would have known he was depressed. I felt I should have known. There was a guilty feeling."

He also felt that somehow he'd been a burden to his father.

Carl's mother says, "He told me that he felt his father's suicide had been caused by the extra burden of having the responsibility for his care."

After his father's death, Carl went to live with his grandmother so he could finish out the school year. Two months later, when he thought his grandmother would be away for the day, Carl took sleeping pills. Fortunately for Carl, though he didn't think so then, his grandmother came home early and found him.

His mother comments, "Carl was starting to have problems in seventh grade, isolating himself from other kids. All he wanted to do was be with his father. Their personalities were very similar. He would just sit with his father in his apartment and watch TV. He did less and less of everything."

On the night Carl's father died, his mother remembers, "his grandmother said he kept calling his father's apartment all night to see if his father would answer. And he kept asking, 'Why did Daddy kill himself in my bathroom?'"

His mother continues, "After Carl took the pills and he was in the hospital, he told me that he'd decided the next time he felt really bad, he was going to die and be with his father."

While his father was alive, Carl had never really been able to have the kind of relationship with him that he'd wanted. Carl had fantasized that through his own suicide, he could accomplish the togetherness he'd never had when his father was alive.

These young people aren't that unusual. Teenage suicide, like suicide at any age, is not new. A 1914 psychological journal reported that "the problem of juvenile suicides has been sensationally exploited in newspapers and numerous brochures for many years. Suicides, like all forms of crime, are becoming more and more precocious."

Although it may not be new, more and more young people today have been attempting suicide. Some of them cannot be rescued in time and they die. Suicide is now one of the leading causes of adolescent death in the nation. The other two are accidents and homicide.

Homicide can be the result of a wish to be killed. A young person who deliberately puts himself in the way of an explosive situation, or provokes an almost certain attack on himself, could be called suicidal. And many "accidents" could well be nonaccidental. A single car crash, especially in conjunction with drug or alcohol use, is another method of suicide that, more often than not, is wrongly classified.

There are reasons for the underreporting and mislabeling of suicides and suicide attempts. One simple explanation is that it's often difficult to know for sure whether the act was deliberate or not.

The more complicated reason behind the unwillingness to call a suicide by its proper name involves ancient history and old fears.

In a book called *The Savage God,* A. Alvarez talks about the reactions of primitive tribes to suicides. Primitive people were terrified of the spirit of the suicide. They believed that a suicide was a strange variety of murder, and therefore must be avenged. The ghost of the suicide would hover about, ready to wreak revenge on a living member of the tribe for the "murder." The suicide's ghost would either destroy his persecutor for him or compel his relatives to carry out the task, or the tribal laws would force the suicide's enemy to kill himself.

With the advent of the religions of Judaism and Christianity, suicide took on the added burden of being a crime against God. It violated the Sixth Commandment, "Thou Shalt Not Kill," and was a blasphemy against the Creator. God, and only God, could give life or take it away.

In the years to follow, suicide and attempted suicide were made criminal acts in many countries, including the United States. As late as 1969, a teenager on the Isle of Man, off the British coast, was ordered by the court to be "birched" (whipped) for attempting suicide.

Furthermore, many people thought that anyone who attempted or died by suicide was insane.

With all of its religious and moral sanctions plus the added onus of insanity, it's no wonder that a family of a suicide or attempted suicide would try to hide the facts. It was and still is a taboo subject that is marked with shame, to be denied, covered up, and, if possible, ignored. Coroners' reports and physicians' files were often altered to read "accident" or "heart failure" to protect the family from gossip. If an attempted suicide was hospitalized, it was, the family said, for an "illness" of some sort, not a suicide attempt. No one wanted a family member to be thought of as crazy.

Society is gradually beginning to talk more about suicide, although ignoring it is still what most people do. The majority of doctors and even mental health workers are uncomfortable dealing with suicidal patients.

Behind our taboo lies a fear of even thinking about suicide. If you talk about it, you will make it happen; don't talk about it, and everything will be okay.

Unfortunately, if a subject is not discussed, rumor, half-truths, and fallacies prevail. Troubled teenagers end up doubly burdened if the topic is taboo: first, by the suicidal state of mind and second, by not being able to talk about it. Experts have shown in case after case that in many young people, the suicidal state of mind was defused after the individuals were able to talk about their feelings.

Take one depressed teenager, add a feeling of not being able to express himself, and mix it with the "normal" state of confrontation between teenager and parents, and it needs only a final spark to push that teenager over the edge.

For the six young people quoted, it happened that way. Relations between them and their parents got worse and problems in school and with friends mounted, until finally these young people felt hopeless. There was no one to go to for help, nowhere to turn, no way to make conditions better. Even caring parents weren't able to communicate their love to their troubled teenagers, or even understand that their children did indeed need help. And what the parents could express wasn't being understood by the children. There was usually a "trigger," too, a final blow that pushed these young people over completely.

All these individuals carried unbearable burdens. They were burdens of anger, guilt, inadequacy, and, most importantly, the burden of not being able to express those emotions in a healthy way. Each was ready for any spark to ignite into a final, self-destructive burst.

But many teenagers feel angry, inadequate, even depressed occasionally and don't attempt or even think about suicide. What is it that makes certain young people do it?

CHAPTER TWO

Truths and Untruths, Signs and Signals

There are many myths, misconceptions, half-truths, and fallacies about suicide. This isn't surprising given the taboos, fears, and stigma that still surround the subject. For the most part, suicide is a topic that people would rather avoid thinking or talking about, as if somehow mentioning it will conjure up the act. The subject of teen suicide has an extra taboo—how it reflects on the parents. After all, if their child killed himself, or tried to, they must somehow be responsible. It must be their fault. They must be bad parents.

Bad parents don't necessarily cause a suicide, although family problems and a lack of communication play major roles in teen depression and suicidal actions. Most parents of suicidal young people do care about them very much. However, if the lines of communication have broken down or parental expectations are unrealistic, the sense of caring can get lost in the midst of the screaming and yelling, or the hurt and angry withdrawal.

The push–pull relationship of the teenager, vital for growth to a healthy adulthood, exacerbates a troubled family relationship. Parents throw up their hands, the teenager feels his parents don't care about him, and nobody talks to anybody else.

If that teenager, who then has to juggle the problems of school, peers, sex, drug and alcohol pressures, doesn't have a secure self-image and a good, strong coping mechanism, he is lost. The end result can be self-destructive behavior.

One myth about suicide is that there is a suicidal type or a suicidal personality. There is no such thing, although there are a number of elements that can contribute to a teenager's being at risk. Although the stereotype is that the "quiet one commits suicide," the "high achiever" or "acting-out" teenager can push himself over the edge, too. Also, although statistics show that more white, middle-to-upper-class suburban teenagers have killed themselves, other groups—the poor, blacks, Hispanics, and urban teenagers—can and do, too.

Another myth about suicidal people is that once the initial depression or suicide attempt is past, the person is well and healthy again and doesn't need to be worried about. This is not true.

There's a certain amount of energy needed to take that final, irrevocable leap to suicide. If a suicidal person's depression seems to have lifted, it may lull those around him into a false security. The initial crisis may be over, but a suicidal person is still ripe for another attempt if there is no monitoring and follow-through by professionals.

This brings us to another myth about suicide—the myth that people who talk about suicide don't do it. Wrong. Sometimes they do.

Suicide threats must be taken seriously. Even if the person is only thinking of the idea, a friend daring him to do it or someone laughing and saying he "must be crazy" to think of such a thing can help turn the thought into reality. A refusal to take the suicidal person's feelings seriously can be the trigger factor, the confirmation that nobody cares or understands. And the anger that is the flip side of the depression can be exacerbated by a dare, such as someone saying, "You wouldn't really do that." That dare can solidify the anger into a final, impulsive action, triggered by thoughts of, "I'll show them."

A suicide or suicide attempt has often been described as a cry for help. It's a message that is sent to significant others, those around the suicidal person who mean a lot in his life—parents, brothers or sisters, friends, a teacher. Many teenagers who attempt suicide, like adults, don't really want to die. They are ambivalent. There is an urge to die, but there is also an urge to live.

That's where prevention, crisis centers, hotlines, peer counseling, and school programs can make the difference between life and death. They can appeal to and make the suicidal young person aware of his positive, life-affirming urges.

If the cry for help is heard, a life can be saved. But we have to know how to listen and what to listen for. To do that, another myth must be dispelled. Contrary to popular misconception, it is not normal for teenagers to be constantly depressed. Ups and downs or mood swings for a day or two or even several days are normal. However, when a teenager is depressed for weeks and doesn't snap out of it, that's a cry for help and a warning sign.

Other red flags include a loss of interest in friends and regular activities, a drop in school grades, changes in eating and sleeping habits, lack of interest in personal appearance, cutting classes, drug and alcohol abuse, constant withdrawal to his or her room, a lack of interest in the future, giving away possessions, and finally a preoccupation with death and talk of suicide.

Most parents of suicidal teenagers say that in retrospect, many of these warning signs were there. They remember that Danny or Susie was frequently up in his or her room every day, wasn't sleeping, wasn't taking care of personal hygiene. And they remember the long, dark days of depression.

A poem written by Lauren six weeks before her suicide attempt illustrates her state of mind then:

wanting so much to be happy
trying so hard to please everyone
never really pleasing yourself
searching for answers among the many faces
always knowing the answers are within
searching and searching
feeling lost and afraid
search ended

CHAPTER THREE
Why?

The scene opens to the sound of an ambulance siren.

"I spent two weeks in the hospital because I tried to kill myself," says the teenage girl. "You see, I couldn't take it anymore. School, my parents' fighting, everybody's always on me. Everything's so hard."

The one person she was able to talk to and feel close to, her boyfriend, has just told her he wants to see other girls. Hurt and angry, she yells at him, "It's either me or other girls." But the argument isn't resolved. Shortly afterward, she sees him with another girl while she's with her girlfriends. They then ask her embarrassing questions about the relationship. Still reeling from the shock, their attitude makes her feel even worse.

"I didn't have anyone to talk to about it. I get all tied in knots when I try to talk about myself. I don't have any close friends. Everyone seems so silly to me. They never talk about anything important."

She begins having difficulty sleeping at night, becoming tired and unable to concentrate in class, where she used to be a good student.

"When I got my grades, I had failed two subjects, and I knew my parents would ground me for a month. The thought of being locked up in that house with them yelling at each other all the time made me sick," she says, her voice rising to a hysterical pitch.

"I was so tired because I could never sleep that one day I fell asleep in class. The teacher caught me and told me to report to the principal. On the way down to his office, I passed the girl's locker room, and I just got out my fingernail file and I...

"Next thing I knew I was in the hospital," she continues. "Now I have to see this shrink once a week. He says that life is sometimes hard, that I've got to keep trying, that I can make it. Maybe he's right. At least now I've got someone to talk to who'll at least listen to what I have to say. Maybe he's right."

Some of the elements involved in teenage suicide are summed up in the above scene performed by a teenage theater group in New Jersey called The Peppermint Players: feeling hopeless about school, a troubled family, problems with friends, and a crisis in a romance.

Suicidal teenagers are sometimes referred to as the vulnerable or the young people at risk. The one thing people agree on is that there is no one theory that explains the growing phenomenon of teenage suicide. However, a number of factors seem to be common among at-risk teens, factors that, if given the right set of circumstances, could put them in jeopardy. The bottom line in most of these factors is a sense of loss.

Death and Divorce: The Feelings of Loss

Loss of a parent, through death or divorce, is considered the leading at-risk element for suicidal teens. As well as feeling abandoned, the young person often experiences a natural anger at the parent who left him. But feeling angry at a parent is guilt-provoking, especially if the parent is dead.

Sylvia Plath, the poet who killed herself when just over thirty, had made several previous attempts. When she was a young child, her father died after a lengthy illness. In her autobiographical novel, *The Bell Jar*, the heroine mourns at her father's grave and then goes home to try to kill herself with a bottle of pills. In a section of one of Plath's poems, "Daddy," she wrote,

> *At twenty, I tried to die*
> *And get back, back, back to you.*
> *I thought even the bones would do.*

The fantasy of rejoining the loved parent can be lethal.

A young individual whose parent commits suicide is said to be at the greatest risk for suicide himself. Not only has he lost a parent, with all the accompanying anger, abandonment, and guilt that go along with it, but he's been taught by his role model that suicide is an acceptable solution to life's difficulties.

Not being able to cope with a parent's death during childhood can lead to an inability to cope with a loss of another relationship during adolescence. The early wounds are reopened, exacerbated, and, if mixed with unresolved guilt, anger, and a sense of abandonment, can lead to suicidal feelings.

Some studies report that as many as 80 percent of suicidal teenagers have had a loss of a parent through death or divorce before reaching the age of fourteen.

Divorce

Nearly all psychologists, mental health counselors, and lawyers agree that the worst problem stemming from today's escalating divorce rate is the effect on children. The same feelings exist here as they do after the death of a parent: anger, abandonment, and guilt.

The scenario of a child of divorce often reads, "If I hadn't been bad, if I'd behaved myself, it wouldn't have happened." What the young person is really saying to himself is, "I'm not worthy enough for my parent's love, so he [or she] left me." Even if he's told he didn't cause the divorce, the feeling that "it's all my fault because I'm not good enough" often remains.

Divorce is usually preceded by long-time hostility. Raising children, like any important aspect of a couple's life, is frequently one of the sources of argument. When the parents finally do separate, therefore, the teenager has even more reason to suspect that he was the cause.

After a divorce, parents should be able to separate their animosity toward each other from their loving feelings and duties as father and mother, but that is rarely the case. Children are frequently made to hear about the "terrible" other parent, and questioned about their loyalty when natural affection for the other parent is shown.

In an article entitled "Children After Divorce: Wounds That Don't Heal," Dr. Judith Wallerstein, who made a ten-year study of children of divorce, stated that adolescence is a period of particularly grave risk for children in divorced families. For most of them, she said, divorce was the single most important cause of enduring pain and anomie in their lives. And, she added, an alarming number of teenagers felt abandoned, physically and emotionally.

The younger a child is when parents divorce, the better that child feels ten years later. This is the case, Dr. Wallerstein said, because younger children do not as often feel responsible for their parents' divorce. Most important, she maintained, is for divorced parents to "give the children permission" to have a relationship with both of them.

However, she and others agree that whenever it happens, divorce always leaves a sense of sadness and loss. And nearly always a young person has the fantasy that somehow his parents will be reunited. Often he thinks he'll be able to get them back together. He may even resort to drastic means to bring father and mother together, such as attempting suicide in the hopes that mutual concern over him will bring about a reconciliation. Not only is his plan doomed to fail, but his suicide attempt may actually succeed.

Up on the high-risk scale with loss of a parent through death or divorce is the feeling of a loss of love from parents.

R. E. Gould, a psychologist, has a theory about how feeling unloved by parents affects a young person. He calls it "the expendable child." The expendable child feels that his parents don't love him and he feels helpless and inadequate. He feels angry at his unloving parents, but can't express it. He feels that his parents never wanted children and would be better off without him. To obtain this longed-for love from his parents, he turns his anger inward, incorporating the "wishes" of his parents to be without his presence, and becoming suicidal.

Suicide has been described as killing off a part of yourself that you don't like. The suicidal person cannot accept some parts of himself and tries to "kill them off."

Karl Menninger, a psychoanalyst, summed up suicide in this way: the wish to kill, the wish to be killed, the wish to die. There is anger against others as well as himself in the suicidal person.

The Anger Turned Inward

Depression is anger turned inward; that is, anger felt toward others and directed toward oneself. Most experts agree that young people, like those of any age who attempt suicide, are often very angry. And although many times a note is written to exonerate family or friends from being "at fault," the note, according to psychiatrist Herbert Hendin, is really an indirect expression of anger toward those whom it is "forgiving."

"In suicide notes," Dr. Hendin states, "such statements specifically freeing particular people of blame and responsibility are usually psychologically read as meaning the opposite." This is a variation of the "you'll-be-sorry-when-I'm-dead" theme.

Nearly all the young people discussed in the first chapter felt very angry. Some of them didn't know why or at whom they were angry. Others did.

Depression

In *Vivienne*, a book about a fourteen-year-old girl who killed herself, Vivienne's older brother and sister both rebelled against their parents with drug and alcohol abuse and sexual experimentation. Vivienne was unable to express her feelings of anger, resentment, and depression to her parents. To them, she presented a bright, cheerful facade.

In the book, one of its authors, Dr. John E. Mack, a professor of psychiatry, says, "One of the most striking aspects of Vivienne's depression was how little of it could be seen in her day-to-day behavior."

This echoes the sentiments of Marilyn's father in the first chapter when he talked about how good kids are at fooling their parents about what's wrong.

This type of behavior, a cover-up of depression, is sometimes called a "masked depression." It's masked with a glossed-over, smooth-surfaced exterior. But these facades often cover up something very lethal—suicidal feelings.

Even if a teenager does express his depressed feelings, far too often they're seen by adults as the normal mood swings of adolescence. "Oh, teenagers are always unhappy, always miserable about something or other" is a common viewpoint. But depression that persists steadily and deeply and is not an isolated, momentary feeling is far from normal. It's an indication that something is seriously wrong.

A teenager who feels depressed will often be fearful of openly expressing these feelings to his parents. First there's the fear of not being taken seriously. Even worse, if he's depressed because he feels his parents don't care about him, he's risking further rejection if he informs them of that. Thus, a vicious cycle is created. Making these feelings known to presumably unloving parents could lead to situations like the following, actually witnessed by psychiatrists.

A teenage girl was having her stomach pumped after a suicide attempt. During the procedure, her mother said, "The next time you decide to do something stupid like this, you ought to use your father's gun."

Dr. Peter Saltzman, a child psychiatrist at McLean Hospital in Massachusetts, related in a magazine interview that a young patient who had tried to commit suicide was told by his father, "Next time, jump off the Bourne Bridge."

In a study of suicidal teens, Dr. Michael L. Peck and Dr. Robert E. Litman reported that not being understood or appreciated by their parents and not being able to express themselves to their parents were a major cause of suicidal feelings. Ninety percent of the young people studied felt their families didn't understand them.

The parent who is too upset or distracted or emotionally needy is incapable of dealing very effectively with the teenager. Even a normally supportive, giving parent can be unavailable emotionally during a death, divorce, financial crisis, or move.

With a consistently needy parent, the parent often sees the young person as an extension of himself or herself. Thus the teenager who's yelled at for not making the varsity team, not being popular with peers, or not making the honor roll is probably supposed to compensate for whatever is missing in the parent's emotional life. Although the parent isn't conscious of this, the message transmitted to the teen is, "I won't love you unless you do, are, or get thus and so."

The Loss of Childhood and Lack of Self-Esteem

"Mattering" is a term used by two psychologists, Morris Rosenberg and B. Claire McCullough, to describe how a teenager's feelings about himself are related to whether he thinks other people care about him. The study found a clear relationship between a teenager's feelings that his parents were interested in and cared about him and his feelings of self-worth.

A loss of self-worth or self-esteem is high on the at-risk list for teenagers. Because the sense of identity is often pretty shaky and fragile during adolescence, feelings of not being worth much in his parents' eyes don't help a young person's self-esteem.

This brings us to a loss that all teenagers must cope with: the loss of childhood. A teenager has to go through a rebirth, recreate himself, between his childhood and adult years. This change from childhood to adulthood is the major upheaval in every life passage. Enormous bodily, mental, and emotional changes occur within this relatively short span of time. Some of these changes may be rapid, others slower, but all in all they keep many young people in a state of disequilibrium.

Together with the newly forming hormonal and growth stages, the teen has to say good-bye to the dependent, not-having-to-be-responsible, often fondly indulged "golden" days of childhood.

This isn't a terrible tragedy, although saying good-bye to anything is hard to do. And, for most young people, adolescence can be an exciting time—a time for growth of ideas, new experiences, exploring a self-image—accompanied by only minor setbacks and annoyances. If, however, the young person carries with him an early loss that has never been resolved, any new crisis he experiences as a teenager can reopen old wounds.

Especially at risk when they become teenagers are those who tried to kill themselves during childhood.

Young children, even preschoolers, can and do attempt suicide. For a long time, people thought it was impossible for a little child to deliberately try to die (as it was long thought impossible for teenagers to be depressed). Young children don't have a sense of the finality of death—how could they be suicidal?

Although it is true that a sense of death doesn't develop until somewhere between ages eight and ten, children can feel so awful about their lives that they "don't want to be here anymore." They are depressed because they feel their parents don't want or love them. Or they may feel "bad"—the cause of their parent's death or a divorce.

According to Dr. Perihan Rosenthal of the University of Massachusetts Hospital, very young children, even two-year-olds, can be suicidal. Most of her cases involved a loss or a separation from a parent. A two-and-a-half-year-old patient tried to get himself run over by a car. He told Dr. Rosenthal, "Nobody loves me. Mommy and Daddy went away because I'm bad and I have to get punished."

Unfortunately, although childhood suicide is being talked about more nowadays, and even dealt with in some cases, many children who attempt suicide aren't treated for it. Their attempt is either attributed to an accident, ignored, or simply avoided in discussion. But what happens to that suicidal child when he becomes a teenager if he's not treated?

Even in a relatively trouble-free childhood, the normal progression to adulthood must bring another loss: loss of childhood's idealized heroes—parents. The childhood vision of these great big adults is of omnipotent gods, superpowerful and infallible. Children need to believe in that image of their parents so they'll feel protected and safe. But equally necessary, for growing up, is the recognition of the idols' shortcomings. The father who "knew everything" doesn't know as much about computers as his teenage daughter. Or Dad's business may have suffered a failure or two that Dad couldn't fix. Mother's supermom image—of wage earner, wife, and all-knowing mother—must lose its glow in her son's mind. The shock of seeing their parents as simply normal, real people, with ordinary pluses and minuses, can be devastating.

Giving up one's gods, or any other childhood fantasy, is sad. A great deal of the ease or difficulty of this vital process depends on family relationships. To grow up in a healthy manner, a young person must be able to pursue his independence from his parents and begin the separation process, while still being able to look behind. He must be allowed one or two last glances backward—for comfort, advice, or perhaps, just for his parents to be there for him.

This is the reason for the "push–pull" attitude of teens. They typically drive their parents crazy with necessary demands for independence. But they also need to sense that they can reach out and touch their parents if they feel insecure, need a bit of propping up, or just to know they are loved.

Insecure Parents = Insecure Children

Some families, however, can't provide security. An "emotionally needy" parent simply isn't capable of meeting the child's needs and, therefore, emotionally neglects or abuses him. And these parents, because of their own problems, discourage communication with their child, which can be crippling.

Dr. Michael Peck, a suicide expert in the Los Angeles area, described what he called a "classic" concept of a typical suicidal teenager.

"It's the young person who comes from insecure parents. They need their kid to make them feel that they're good parents by telling them how well everything's going, even if it means their kid must lie to them. The message is, 'Just tell me the good stuff.' The kids learn not to communicate, and the tendency not to communicate spills over into other relationships and friendships. They don't talk about their problems. They don't communicate with adults or peers. They're afraid of their negative thoughts and feelings. As they move into their midteens, they become more isolated from everyone. He or she is not really growing up because there's no way to grow up or to do things other kids are doing. That's when they become hopelessly suicidal and feel that they are never going to be 'normal.'"

Dr. Vincent Fontana, who has worked with abused children in New York City, comments, "Many suicidal teenagers live in an 'emotional refrigerator.' There's no loving, no caring. Every day it's, 'Eat your breakfast, here's lunch, dinner, do your homework,' but not sitting down and really talking. Most parents think communication is telling the child what to do. But communication," he says, "means talking and listening."

Physical abuse is another horrendous reality in today's

society. When a young person is physically abused, the abuse can cause so much emotional pain that the only escape the victim can see is death.

Dr. Fontana remarks, "When the abuse gets to the point of being intolerable, they turn to drugs, alcohol, and eventually to suicide, because nobody really cares."

In a study of fifty abused children and their families who had undergone treatment in several New York hospitals, Dr. Arthur Green reported that abused youngsters frequently clung to their identification as victims and reenacted their parents' hostility toward them. They acted self-destructively, which, he stated, "represented the child's compliance with parental wishes for his or her destruction and/or disappearance."

Sexual abuse is one of the most traumatic forms of child abuse. With girls, both children and teenagers, the abuser is often a member of the family or household. It could be a father or stepfather, a mother's boyfriend, an uncle or a grandfather. Frequently the victim is threatened with reprisals if she "tells." Even if she gets up the courage to tell someone, many times no one believes her. Or worse, she's made to feel that she "asked" for it. The effects of the abuse are then multiple. There is the victimization itself, the burden of carrying this "shameful" secret, and the feeling of monstrous betrayal by the adult who, instead of protecting and nurturing her, abuses her.

Sexual abuse often leads to confusion about her sexual development. It can prompt her to run away, to turn to prostitution, or to end up a suicide.

With boys, sexual abuse usually comes from outside the home and family, that is, from a "trusted" father figure such as a teacher, a scout leader, a clergyman, a coach. The same problems and effects of the abuse are as true for boys as for girls, including suicide.

For example, a twelve-year-old boy from Emerson, New Jersey, killed himself by drinking liniment. According to his parents, he chose to die because he had been sexually molested by a Franciscan priest during a scout camp session.

Although this type of victimization cannot be overstated, an even more common type of abuse is the already discussed emotional abuse and neglect.

Dr. Fontana remarks, "Some of these kids have been given everything, materially. But they didn't get the feeling of really being wanted, really being part of the family unit."

Rabbi Daniel Roberts, of Temple Emanuel in Cleveland, states, "Viewing their kids as status symbols rather than human beings, parents all too often neglect to express love, listen to their children's problems, or support them during trying times."

Rabbi Roberts, who produced a film on teenage suicide, cautioned parents not only about emotional neglect, but also about the pressures they put on their children to succeed.

The Pressure for Success

Achievement in school is one of the biggest sources of communication problems, anxiety, and friction between teens and parents as well as between teens and their peers. Some of the unrealistic expectations of both teens and parents in this area can lead to disaster.

School takes up most of a teenager's time and energy. This is where skills, scholastic and social, are practiced, tested, and honed daily. The amount and importance of what happens during those five days each week can be compared with what happens to an adult in his on-the-job, marital, and social situations.

Everything's okay if the young person makes the basketball team, passes his math exam, gets the part he wants in the play, if the girl he likes likes him. But if one or more of these things don't happen, all too often the young person considers himself a failure.

School problems like learning disabilities are now recognized by psychologists as leading "at-risk" factors in young people. It's not the disability itself, but the years of frustration over not being able to keep up with and being teased by classmates that can bring a learning-disabled young person to the brink of despair, especially if he doesn't get any help or support.

Young people who don't suffer learning problems can feel just as pressured in school if they have unreasonably high standards they try to live up to. They can feel like failures if they don't make "As" or don't get accepted into a particular college.

A quote from a student in a report from the White House Conference on Children in 1970 reads, "If I ever commit suicide, I'll leave my school schedule behind as a suicide note."

Psychologist Martha Haldopoulos, of New Jersey, comments, "If a former 'A' student becomes a 'C' student, that's grounds for suicidal thoughts, right there. It's a terrible loss of identity."

In a television documentary called "College Can Be Killing," about the problems college students face, producer Michael Hirsh concluded that large, anonymous institutions made students feel alienated. These students, especially freshmen, already felt uprooted, lonely, and under intense academic and social pressure.

In the documentary, a student from Northwestern University said, "I was worried about how I was doing and what my parents had given up to put me through school. And I would speak with my parents and they would tell me that 'we gave all this up to put you through school.' I'd say, 'Yes, mother.' And they'd say, 'You'd better be getting 'As' or we'll be wasting our money,' and it would make me get pretty depressed."

As many as one-quarter of college freshmen will consider or act out suicidal feelings, according to Dr. Javad H. Kashani, a University of Missouri professor of psychiatry. He and Marybeth Priesmeyer surveyed 725 clients at a liberal arts college counseling service.

"The freshmen are coming from childhood to young adulthood," Dr. Kashani said in his report. "They must make a role change quickly. They are away from home, away from their families, away from many of their friends. Their parents are paying for their studies and, for the first time, there is a real chance that they could flunk out. All of these make life very stressful."

To show further how a stressful school situation can lead to teenage suicide, it's interesting to look at the culture of Japan. The terrible stress Japanese teenagers undergo during examinations was studied by Dr. Mamoru Iga as one of the factors contributing to the high Japanese teenage suicide rate—one of the highest in the world.

"Probably the most important cause of stress among Japanese youth is the examination system, which is often referred to as 'Examination Hell,'" reported Dr. Iga.

The school system in Japan, he said, "is do-or-die." There is only one road, the examinations, for any future achievement and success as an adult. The entrance examination to the university is the single most important event in the life of a young Japanese. Preparing for it begins in early childhood with much memorizing and long exercises and drill. If a young person doesn't get into one of the "better" universities because of low scores, he may be sent to a "cram school." Then his parents must pay to keep him in what sometimes must be a boarding situation if they live far from the school, even if they can ill afford it.

"If the student then fails, under such conditions, his sense of guilt may be overwhelming," said Dr. Iga.

There are other cultural factors in Japan that contribute to the high teen suicide rate: extreme competitiveness; status differences; a value on delaying gratification and enduring hardship; the family structure; and the societal-religious attitude toward suicide.

Sex discrimination against women in Japan is still very strong. A woman who is a wife and mother is expected to make her husband and children her center of existence. Frustrated by lack of opportunities for herself, the Japanese mother pushes her child to achieve, which is expected of her. In Japan, children, like adults, are not permitted to express hostile feelings. Thus it would be unthinkable for a child to show anger toward his pressuring mother, even when her expectations for him are unrealistic.

All these factors—educational, familial, cultural—contribute to Japan's increasing youth suicide rate.

In Truk, a group of Micronesian islands, there is a drastically increasing teen suicide rate. Among young males between the ages of fifteen and twenty-four, there are now twenty-five deaths for every ten thousand.

According to anthropologists who've been studying this, one reason is the "Westernization" of the traditional culture. This has caused the erosion of the tight family structure and old values, especially that of the parent–child relationship. Another factor is that the youth in these islands, like the

Japanese, don't feel comfortable about expressing anger with their families. These factors must inevitably contribute to young people's seeing suicide as a way out.

Cultural and Sexual Factors

In our own society, there are cultural differences that influence variations in teen suicide statistics.

The suicide rate for white, middle-class male teenagers is much higher than that for blacks; and for blacks, higher than for Hispanics. According to Dr. Michael Peck, Hispanics have a lower suicide rate than other teenagers primarily because of family closeness, although many teens experience problems because of the conflict of the Spanish cultural values of their parents and those of today's American youth.

American Indian young adults—as well as this population in general—have a high suicide rate. This is a result of the erosion of native traditional values and the lack of self-esteem in Indian society in white America.

Suicide rates among poorer teenage blacks are relatively low because of strong family and cultural traditions, but once young black males become adults and seek acceptance into the socioeconomic world of America, their suicide rates climb. There are several reasons for this.

Young adult black men who have moved away from family and community traditions frequently have nowhere to turn if they are confronted by racism and lack of job opportunities. They may internalize stress and be reluctant to display anger.

"When young blacks begin to internalize personal frustrations and failures, and no longer use the traditional institutional structures, relationships, and groups within the black community to shield them, there is an increase in the likelihood of self-destruction," said Robert Davis, in a report on suicide among young adult blacks.

The difference in suicide statistics between boys and girls is changing. Traditionally, three times as many girls as boys tried to kill themselves. And three times as many boys died. The methods teenage girls used were thought of as more feminine and passive ones—pills and wrist-slitting. Boys, on the other hand, usually used more masculine, or violent methods—shooting, stabbing, jumping, hanging. These have less chance of rescue.

But, as the sexes are becoming more equal, the resulting statistics for girls are unfortunately increasing.

Conversely, however, perhaps the growing equality will have a positive effect on boys. Traditionally, girls have felt more able to talk about their feelings, including depression and suicide. Boys have not felt "permitted" to discuss feelings openly in our culture, especially if those feelings implied weakness. Boys have also been discouraged from becoming really close, in terms of being able to talk, to other boys, whereas girls have usually confided their deepest thoughts to their best friends.

Discussing suicide with a friend who understands may help alleviate deep problems and get the person into counseling. If boys are able to be more open about their feelings, there will be a lot less pressure to bear their problems alone.

Today's sexual pressures, said Dr. John Mack in his story of Vivienne, can be terribly destructive to young people entering their teens. Dr. Mack feels that our present-day culture pushes teens into sexual relationships they are often not ready for and can't handle emotionally.

At age thirteen, Vivienne was reportedly terrified of the thought of sex and of the young men making advances to her.

Dr. Sol Gordon, an expert on teenage sexuality, says that fear of, or actual, pregnancy is the largest single factor in teenage girls' attempting or committing suicide. In many cases, he says, the attempt or the suicide is precipitated by abandonment by the boy involved. She is often rejected by her family, too. With nowhere to turn and frightened by the responsibility of a child, a pregnant teenager could easily become suicidal.

Melissa Putney, from rural Maryland, and nine months pregnant, lay down on a railroad track and waited for a train to kill her. It did. She had written a note to her mother saying, "You always asked me if there's anything wrong. I said, 'No, I'm okay.' Mom, I wasn't telling the truth. I was never okay. I was very depressed."

Melissa wouldn't admit to anyone, even herself, that she was pregnant. Weeks before she killed herself, she wrote in her diary, "I am not pregnant."

Because there has traditionally been a double standard in our culture about sex, there's usually less pressure on boys than girls. But boys, too, can be damaged by feeling pushed into relationships they're not emotionally ready for—because "everyone's doing it."

Sexual identities can cause confusion and anxiety during teenage years when they are still being formed. Probably the biggest fear for a young person is whether he or she is "normal" sexually. There is also often a concern over homosexuality, real or imagined.

"People have reported incidents of young men attempting or actually committing suicide because of fears of homosexuality," says Dr. Gordon. "There's a lot of clinical data on that. It's a heavy trip for boys, since it's considered such a stigma."

What is "normal" also affects other aspects of a teenager's life. Normal, in terms of what his or her peers find acceptable, can weigh heavily on a young person's mind. Being accepted and liked by classmates, or a group of people one's own age, means the difference between feeling part of life or "out of it." And the more isolated and alienated the individual feels, the more depressed he is and the lower the sense of self-esteem.

Peer Groups and Isolation

Peers are enormously important to young people. They are a part of every young person's forging of an identity, which is helped along by those like oneself. The teenager is moving from the sense of himself instilled in him by his parents to that which he receives from his friends. If there are no friends, or if the sense of one's self from other teens isn't a good one, self-esteem plummets.

Says Dr. Peter Giovacchini, a psychiatrist, "No longer able to cling to their parents as they once did, a teen's peer group often takes on the importance of a life jacket buoying him up. But this life-saving peer group itself is composed of members who are all relatively insecure."

Insecure or not, feeling accepted and comfortable among other teens is vital to a sense of identity and well-being. One of the most devastating things that can happen to a teenager is losing his peer support and having to make a whole new place for himself, when the family moves, for instance.

"Moving," says psychologist Martha Haldopoulous, who specializes in helping families cope with adjustments of corporate relocation, "involves the same type of emotional losses for teens as death or divorce."

A study she conducted in Park Ridge, a suburb of Chicago, with teenagers who had recently moved revealed that "no kid said it was easy or 'no problem,'" she reported. "The most important thing to them was to be able to find a friend as an opening to the new situation."

Teenagers in her study felt multiple losses: their room, their home, pets, boyfriend/girlfriend, friends, school, and sense of territory. With teens who'd moved several times, each move made it more difficult to adjust.

A considerable number had considered suicide. And most of them had been frequently depressed.

They're angry, because they don't feel they had any say in the move or choice. They feel as if they've been kidnapped.

Transferring credentials, whether as captain of the football team or first violinist in the orchestra, is terrifying. They wonder, "What will I be there?" All of the accomplishments they've accrued and all of their identity that goes along with them have to be transferred.

There can also be a problem with schoolwork. If class structure, content, and standards were different at the old school, an "A" student from one high school can find himself getting "Cs" in his new school. And that's an added pressure.

Plano, a suburb of Dallas, suffered a rash of teen suicides in 1983. Plano went through a rapid growth period, increasing in population from eleven thousand to ninety thousand in just ten years. Judie Smith, who has worked with suicidal teenagers in Dallas, feels that the transplantation of families and the rootlessness teenagers felt contributed greatly to the wave of suicides.

"The major factor, the common thread," she remarks, "is the experience of loss. These kids have lost friendships, ties—it's a traumatic upheaval when a child is moved from one community to another. Mostly they moved from out-of-state. Some had moved more than once. And," she adds, "once they get through this and there's another loss, like a breakup of a relationship with a boyfriend or girlfriend, it's an added crisis. These kids haven't had the life experience to get over it."

In today's society most families don't stay put the way previous generations did. The mobile family has almost become an American way of life.

The mobile family, the single-parent family, the school and peer and sexual pressures on today's teens have to be coped with. And teenagers also have to learn to cope with what society will offer them as adults.

Will There Be a Future?

A surprising number of teenagers surveyed in high schools in northern New Jersey revealed their worries about the possibility of a nuclear war. The survey was conducted by a group called Physicians for Social Responsibility.

Dr. Donald Louria, of the northern New Jersey group, says that teenagers need to believe in their future.

"With an unstable society and no confidence in the future, there's likely to be an increase in suicides," he says.

Teenagers are usually idealistic and need a world they can believe in. They need to feel there's a meaningful life to look forward to when they become adults. They need to be able to cope with that life in a realistic, fulfilling manner.

According to Dr. Harold Treffert, director of the Winnebago Mental Health Institute of Oshkosh, Wisconsin, "A lot of teenage suicides are the result of the 'American Fairy Tale.'" He defines this as, "More possessions means happiness; a person who produces is more important; everyone must belong to or identify with a larger group; perfect mental health means no problems; a person is abnormal unless he or she is constantly happy."

Not being able to cope with stress and pain is one of the key factors in teenage suicide.

Rabbi Daniel Roberts comments, "It is our job to help

young people learn that pain is part of life. It can be dealt with and overcome. Nothing is hopeless."

Judie Smith of Dallas remarks, "It's very difficult for a young person to come to grips with realizing that life is going to be joyful again after a crisis. We're trying too hard to protect our kids from pain and disappointment. Because of that protection, they don't learn how to cope. You learn from stress."

A study of high schoolers in Connecticut by Dr. Alexander Tolor, reported in the *New York Times*, showed wide differences in what high schoolers feel is stressful—and what adults think high schoolers think. Teenagers rated having to go to summer school, being suspended from school, and doing badly on college entrance exams as very stressful. Teachers and psychologists hadn't seen these factors as particularly stressful for teens at all.

"These kids might be laboring under stress and turmoil we do not appreciate," Dr. Tolor said in the interview. "What we might be seeing is adults basing their assumptions on what they find important or stressful in their own lives."

The "time warp" factor plays a heavy role in stress and depression. It's difficult for a young person to realize that today's very real and seemingly insoluble problems and pain will not go on forever.

It's not that the breakup of a romance, the low grade on an exam, or not getting into the right college aren't very real, painful situations—they are. And a parent, another adult, or even a friend saying, "Big deal," doesn't help—it makes it worse. This lack of understanding and denial of the reality of the hurt and disappointment only contribute to the despair.

Adolescence is probably the best—and worst—time in most people's lives. From the young men and women who suffer only minor bumps and bruises along the path to those who feel so bad at times they think they'd rather be dead, it's a fairly rocky road. It has to be. From the safe, warm, protected world of childhood, growing young people have to find out who they are, cope with physical and emotional ups and downs, learn to take care of themselves, and leave their parents.

The "Missing" Link

Given all of the pressures teenagers confront today, we still must go back to the last sentence in Chapter One: What makes certain teenagers want to die?

All the variables discussed here are certainly part of the problem of teenage suicide. But most young people do manage to cope with their lives and do not turn to suicide. What is the "x" factor?

The missing ingredient here is the particular personality of the young person himself.

Dr. Fontana says, "I think there's a particular profile of a child who, because of his environment, will either act out or remain repressed. There is a combination of genetic factors, family, and environment. And if you've got that potential there, and the self-esteem is low, you've got a suicidal child."

Many young people can weather a divorce, a move, a drop in grades, and a broken relationship. They will feel bad for a while, then pick themselves up again. Others can't.

Some psychiatrists and psychologists believe that there is a certain biological or chemical imbalance in some young people that would tend to make them more likely to get severely depressed. Heredity, too, plays a part. If a parent is very depressed, there can be a genetic tendency for a young person to be that way also.

A lack of coping skills could be used to describe Vivienne's predicament. She was portrayed in the book as especially sensitive from her early childhood. She was so sensitive to other people's pain that their hurt actually caused her pain, too. Things that might not bother other people would deeply affect her. She was highly idealistic and suffered when she and the rest of the world did not live up to those ideals.

Another kind of vulnerability that is frequently found in suicidal young people is the need to be "perfect." The teenager who is a "perfect" student, who doesn't give his parents any "trouble," and who is the "good boy" is often very troubled.

Some teenagers, when they are angry or hurt, rebel or act out their feelings. Others, however, cannot express those feelings. They turn their hurt and anger inward, and self-destruct.

CHAPTER FOUR

Other
Self-Destructive
Behavior

In addition to actual suicide attempts, there are other ways teenagers end up hurting themselves. Some of these methods are slow and subtle. Some aren't even noticed by family or friends for years.

When drinking and drugs, for example, take over a young person's life, becoming its focal point, this can certainly be considered suicidal behavior. The end of the road can be death.

Many types of self-destructive behavior have the same roots as suicide: a lack of self-esteem, an inability to cope, depression, feeling unloved, and a sense of loss.

If an individual feels that he's no good and nobody cares about him, then it doesn't seem to matter what he does to his body or mind.

The Quick Fix

At the top of the list for slow demolition are drug and alcohol abuse.

The typical downhill spiral begins like this. A teenager gets lonely, frustrated, anxious, and angry. He looks for something to "take the pain away." Some experts refer to this as "self-medication," or seeking a "quick fix." It's not surprising that teens turn to this method of problem-solving. They see adults everywhere popping pills and downing drinks to solve their problems.

The trouble with a quick fix is that it's just that. It's a momentary cover-up for something that requires a real solution. And the quick fix creates its own problems, too. Not only doesn't it cure the depression, anger, or loneliness, but it layers new problems on top of the original ones— problems created by chemical dependency. Drug and alcohol dependency eventually take over the young person's life, leaving him even less able to cope with his feelings than before he started taking his "medication."

The reason for self-medication, psychologists say, is because a troubled young person doesn't want to feel anything. Feelings are painful, and the teenager feels helpless about doing anything about the problems causing the pain. He doesn't think he has permission to express these feelings. He may be laughed at. His parents may think he's making a big deal out of nothing. His friends might not understand. His parents may be so wrapped up in their own problems that he perceives he can't burden them with his.

Slow debilitation of the body due to long-term drug abuse can lead to death. So can disease contracted by using dirty needles, or taking a mixture of drugs. Drugs can also kill by overdose. Taking one, two, or three times the amount the body can absorb for a bigger high can create a high one never comes down from. Sometimes the o.d. isn't an accident, but a final push down the long slide toward death.

According to Chinita Fulchon, a social psychologist who has worked with teenagers at The Door, a help center in New York, "Studies show that 50 percent of adolescents who attempt suicide are under the influence of drugs or alcohol at the time. A suicide attempt may occur under these circumstances because the use of drugs and alcohol tends to lower the controls that inhibit behavior."

Most experts do not believe that drug or alcohol abuse in and of itself directly causes suicide attempts. What they do believe is that in addition to being a form of self-destruction, drugs and alcohol impair functioning and thinking. This impairment, combined with depression, anger, or suicidal feelings, can act as the trigger that pushes the teen over the edge.

Drugs and alcohol can also be a trigger in auto accidents and fatalities. In fact, single-car crashes are sometimes called "autocides" because they appear to be intentionally self-destructive. Usually, autocides happen after drinking or drug use.

After a long period of feeling angry or depressed, a young person drinks heavily or takes drugs with friends or at a party. Maybe there's an argument with a parent, friend, or girlfriend. He rushes out the door, gets behind the wheel, and guns the motor. Thoughts like "I'll show them" or "They'll be sorry" run through his head as he races the car. Then there's a head-on collision with a pole or a tree, or a plunge over an embankment.

Dr. Joseph Novello, who has worked with young people at The Gateway, a treatment program for teen drug abusers, reports, "When you add up the numbers, you come to the chilling conclusion that drugs and alcohol, in tandem, are probably the leading cause of death among American teenagers. For example, accidental death is the leading cause of mortality among adolescents, but we know that sixteen thousand youngsters in a recent year died in alcohol-related fatalities."

Taking Fatal Risks

Reckless driving is one form of risk-taking behavior that is self-destructive. Risk-taking behavior that could knowingly lead to injury or death can take other forms; for example, self-mutilation such as cutting or burning one's skin.

Peter became very depressed after his family moved East from California. He made no friends in his new school. He was convinced that no one liked him.

He changed schools again, this time to an academically demanding private school. With the mounting pressure of schoolwork, he got more depressed and angry. When he was feeling very troubled, Peter would cut himself with his fingernails. He'd dig deep into his hands and arms. And he'd smash his knuckles into walls.

"When I had to make myself bleed, I'd go take it out on the walls," he recalls.

One of Peter's arms bears angry scars where he set it on fire with a cigarette lighter.

"A lot of times I get angry about things and then I just feel like hurting myself. Whenever my dad's name comes up, for instance," he says. "My dad expects me to be perfect."

Other kinds of self-destructive behavior are more outward. These can range from fights with parents to truancy and disciplinary problems in school.

Much of this acting-out behavior could be classified as "normal" teenage rebellion. The very word rebellion, used to describe the goings on between teens and parents, implies something revolutionary and tumultuous.

If parents are able to weather this trying behavior and show they still care for their child underneath the unacceptable hairstyle, clothes, music, and friends, then the teenager remains relatively secure. He can explore the world, even fight furiously with his parents about politics, morals, religion, without worrying about loss of love and acceptance while he forges his identity.

But if parents aren't able to relax some of the standards they have set for their son or daughter, if the home atmosphere is so rigid that there's no room for the young person to grow and still feel accepted, the wheels are set in motion for a self-destructive cycle.

Normal acting-out can then turn into alcoholism, drug abuse, delinquency, or more violent behavior.

What lies underneath violent behavior can be a wish to die. Putting oneself in the middle of a known life-threatening situation is certainly provocative behavior. Underneath this behavior must be a wish for self-destruction. This way, someone else "does the job."

This is what happens in the movie *West Side Story*. Tony, the white gang hero, thinks his girlfriend, Maria, who is affiliated with the rival Puerto Rican gang, is dead. He feels that he has nothing to live for. He walks out—undefended, unarmed, alone—into the rival gang territory. He shouts to Chino, his rival for Maria's affection, to come and get him. Chino obliges and shoots him.

Running away from home is another type of acting-out behavior that may result in suicide. Most young people who leave home are trying to get away from an unpleasant, hard-to-bear situation. But if the runaway finds himself hungry and sleeping on the streets, it's not a solution. And this could ultimately lead to a suicide or suicide attempt.

Sexual Acting Out

A young girl who ends up as a prostitute may also have made a conscious decision to pursue it.

Teenage boys and girls who have been sexually abused by family members or trusted adults are especially vulnerable to acting out promiscuous sexual behavior. They may feel guilty somehow of provoking the sexually abusive behavior. As adolescence approaches, the sexual feelings of abuse victims are often very confused. The one thing nearly all victims have in common is a feeling of worthlessness. One way of acting out this feeling is by becoming "anybody's" sexual partner. Through promiscuity or prostitution, they're treating their bodies the way they were treated by those who were entrusted with their love and care.

Starving to Death

Much of the self-destructive or risk-taking behavior discussed above could be described as active.

There is another life-threatening behavior that is more aptly described as passive. This is anorexia nervosa. Anorexia is often referred to as the "starvation disease" because it is characterized by eating little or nothing until its victim nearly or finally dies.

The anorectic is usually a teenage girl or young woman from a middle-class background where the family expects a great deal from their children. What often starts out as an ordinary diet can become a compulsion. It ends up controlling the young woman's life, and can cause her death. One reason for this is society's obsession with thin female bodies, which is especially promoted by the media.

But the more complicated reasons exist for this drastic illness than our cultural "thin is in" bias. One factor may be a young girl's fear of her budding sexuality, of growing up and becoming a woman. The anorectic is usually the "good girl," the "compliant one," the "perfectionist." She shares many characteristics with the overtly suicidal teenagers. She cannot express her overwhelming anger toward her parents openly. She feels they control her life, so she decides to control the one thing she can—her own body.

A young woman goes on a starvation diet, eating literally nothing. At meals with her parents, she'll pretend she's eating, or lie, saying she's already eaten. To help the process along, she exercises violently. She'll get up at dawn to run or bicycle for miles or swim dozens of laps in a pool until she is exhausted. She'll use diuretics and laxatives to further her "progress." If she does eat, it's never in moderation. Rather, she'll binge, then force herself to throw up. This form of the illness is called bulimia.

Another aspect of this disease is the anorectic's obsession with recipes and cooking. Part of her compulsive behavior is a love–hate relationship with food. She pores over recipes and cooks up a storm, but doesn't eat a bite. She'll spend hours making elaborate concoctions for her family. She'll make scrapbooks of recipes and paste pictures of food on the walls of her room. Nevertheless, when she looks in her mirror, she sees only a fat person. Even after she's starved herself down to 80 pounds, which anorectics often do, she doesn't see skin and bones. She sees rolls of blubbery fat.

The more her parents tell her she's wasting away, the more they beg her to eat, the more she resists. It's a deadly game, however, because she can suffer permanent organic damage even if she lives through the ordeal. If she finally gets help, the whole family often has to be treated because it's a family problem.

A former victim of anorexia who nearly died, Cherry Boone O'Neill, wrote about her ten-year struggle in her book, *Starving for Attention*.

The eldest of four daughters of singer Pat Boone, she was the "good girl," the one who was "no trouble," who thought she had to be "perfect." She also felt very controlled by her family. She writes:

> *And why had I developed an eating disorder in the first place? Obviously, there had been unfulfilled emotional needs in my life. The need for acceptance and approval— the need to be perfect—had been a driving force that ultimately brought me to the brink of death. In my early years, I equated my worth as a person with the level of my performance and I felt the love and approval of other people would be conditional upon my perfection. Therefore, I expended every effort to be the best I could possibly be in any given area of endeavor, only to repeatedly fall short of my goals and risk losing value in the eyes of others. Trying even harder, only to miss the mark again and again, resulted in compounded guilt and self-hatred.*

The book includes some insights of Cherry's therapist about her condition:

> *"Tell me, Cherry, why is it that you want to die?" asks Dr. Raymond E. Vath ... "You see, anorexia nervosa may be seen as a slow form of suicide. Although it can begin as a socially acceptable attempt to lose weight, the fear of rejection and guilt over imperfections create a depression and a suicidal plunge that are very difficult to come out of. The potentially lethal partnership of deep depression and low self-esteem is a powerful one."*

Cherry Boone O'Neill eventually regained her health through therapy. But Karen Carpenter, the popular singer, did not. She died of a heart attack at the age of thirty-two. According to experts, including Dr. Vath, her death was the result of the strain on her heart from years of anorexia.

Karen, too, grew up with high expectations of herself, was known as a "cheerful, helpful" type of person, and is said to have had a strict family background. For years, she struggled with the disease, looking much of the time like a skeleton. During her struggle, she talked to Cherry Boone O'Neill, admitting her need for help. Finally, she went for treatment at a hospital and brought her weight up from 85 to 108 pounds, normal for her height. But it wasn't in time.

Though the majority of anorectics and bulimics are young women, some are male. Sometimes young men will go on starvation diets encouraged by their sports coaches in order to "weigh in" at a more competitive weight for, say, a wrestling team. But most male anorectics, like their female counterparts, have a feeling of a lack of control over their lives, anger at their parents, and a low self-image.

Peter, whom we talked about earlier, first tried to destroy himself, slowly, with anorexia.

"It was a type of suicide," says Peter. "It started when I was 13 and got worse. I didn't want to be fat. I thought I was. So I just decided to start watching myself. First, I just ate whatever I wanted and exercised. Then I started exercising more and eating less. I realized that if I didn't eat more and kept exercising, I'd lose weight.

"The beginning of that summer, I got down to 115 pounds. [Peter is 5′ 5″ tall.] I was swimming 300 laps, riding my bike five miles, doing 1000 sit-ups, push-ups, working out on the nautilus—tons of things."

And, he noted with grim satisfaction, "My father, he'd always be, like— 'I want you to gain weight. I want you to gain weight.' Every time he'd say that, I'd just say, "damn you"—and I just lost weight."

Because the drastic weight loss landed him in a hospital and didn't kill him, he began mutilating himself until he finally received treatment for his self-destructive behavior.

Peter is a good example of the fact that, at bottom, much self-destructive behavior is symptomatic of the same underlying problems shared by many young people. The only difference is that because of the individual personality or circumstances, one troubled young person seeks one way out, another, a different but equally lethal way. Although none of the various acts described in this chapter are technically "suicidal," they are self-destructive and dangerous. And they can—and do—kill.

CHAPTER FIVE

Suicide

in the

Media

In *Romeo and Juliet*, two star-crossed teenage lovers separated by a family feud end up by killing themselves. Since even before Shakespeare's time, romantic love in literature and drama has often been associated with death. Many times, lovers planned to be "reunited in death."

If love goes sour or is suddenly unavailable, a love-and-death movie or book can be a "trigger factor" for a problem-plagued teenager. The deaths of movie and rock idols can also be trigger factors for troubled young people. Experts say that after John Lennon was shot and after Marilyn Monroe died, there was an increase in youth suicides. This is due to an overly strong identification with the dead idol, possibly a romantic fantasy, combined, of course, with serious problems in the young person's life.

They'll Be Sorry When I'm Gone

There is also the fantasy of "watching others cry at my funeral," or making oneself into a "romantic" figure by dying—like Johnny, in Chapter One. The obvious flaw in this reasoning is that the young person won't be around to see his friends' reactions at his funeral.

The "you'll be sorry when I'm dead" threat that some teenagers angrily yell at their parents ends the same way. The parents will indeed be sorry, but the teenager won't be around to get any sense of comfort from it.

In *You'll Miss Me When I'm Gone*, by Stephen Roos, sixteen-year-old Marcus tries to cope with his parents' divorce, an uncommunicative father, and a mother who drinks too much—by drinking himself. Drinking worsens his problems: drunk, he totals the car; his girlfriend breaks up with him because of his drinking; he can't deal with classmates or concentrate on schoolwork; and he's in danger of losing his prized position on the school paper.

Feeling worse and worse, he drinks more and more. He has blackouts, gets violent, wrecks the living room. He tells his father, "Next time I may run someplace where people don't come back from." (He disappeared overnight once before.) He makes "jokes" about suicide to the school psychiatrist. Finally, he writes a letter to the school paper's advice columnist about how unhappy he is and how angry he is with his parents, ending with, "By the time you read it, I'll be far away. You'll miss me when I'm gone."

He tells himself that it "would have been better for everyone if he'd been as totaled as his car." When no one is home that night, be begins a massive drinking bout. But the alcohol doesn't have enough effect for him. So he swallows a bunch of his mother's tranquilizers. Woozy, he suddenly realizes that he might not make it and he admits to himself that he "didn't want to die. Not now. Not this way." (Most suicide attempts and self-destructive acting-out are ambivalent.) Luckily, his family finds him and gets him to a hospital in time. He takes the first step toward getting help by acknowledging that he has a drinking problem. And he's looking forward to living his life.

Clusters of Dying

In the book *Suicide in America*, author Herbert Hendin tells the story of the mayor of a town where a number of young women were killing themselves. He tried stopping the deaths by issuing a proclamation that the naked body of any suicide would be displayed in the public square. It seemed to have the instantaneous effect of decreasing the numbers of young women committing suicide.

The story, Mr. Hendin believes, rests on the theory that a suicidal person may be concerned with how he or she imagines feeling after death.

"The mayor," Mr. Hendin stated, "had the sense to disapprove of and demythologize suicide."

Demythologizing, deglamorizing, and deromanticizing suicide can be a lifesaver.

According to Abraham Matus, a suicide specialist and psychologist at Ridgewood High School in New Jersey, "Some schools have been stupid enough to have memorial services for a suicide student. We feel very strongly that in no way should you memorialize suicide, because it then becomes an opening for someone else—because of the attention and the 'glamour' of it."

During the winter of 1978, two teenagers committed suicide in one week in Ridgewood, an upper-middle-class suburb. Around the same time, Berkeley Heights, another well-to-do New Jersey suburb, suffered a similar phenomenon. In Cherry Creek, a suburb of Denver, Colorado, four junior and senior high schoolers died in an eighteen-month period in 1980 and 1981. In 1983, ten teenagers from the northern suburbs of New York City killed themselves. In 1983 and 1984, the North Dallas area—including Plano, North Dallas, Richardson, Mesquite, and Garland—counted twenty-two youth suicides. In suburban Seattle, four junior and senior high schoolers killed themselves within several months in 1985. In 1986, three students in an Omaha high school committed suicide in less than two weeks.

And in 1987, in Bergenfield, New Jersey, four young people—two sisters and two young men—formed a suicide pact and died. Several days later, in a Chicago suburb, two young women died together in the same manner.

Some people refer to a number of deaths in the same area within a short period of time as "clusters." The "epidemic" or "contagious" nature—if it exists—of teenage suicide is being debated and investigated by experts throughout the country. How much effect does one teenage suicide have on others? What, if anything, is the contagious effect? Why are there clusters?

The Centers for Disease Control (CDC) in Atlanta has been studying clusters of teen suicides to get some answers. In 1987, representatives from the CDC met with members of nine communities in the country that had experienced youth suicide clusters.

The CDC report states that suicide clusters in general, whether multiple simultaneous suicides or a series of suicides occurring close together in time and space, may account for no more than 1 to 5 percent of all youth suicides. But, the report adds, the imitative suicides suggest that suicide may have a contagious effect: other young people had died from unnatural causes before the identified cluster, and these deaths may have influenced the young people involved in the cluster of suicides. For example, in the nine months preceding one cluster of four suicides and two suicide attempts among fifteen- to twenty-four-year-olds, there were four traumatic deaths in the community among people in the same age group: at least one of these deaths was suicide.

The CDC concludes that those at high risk for suicide clusters include relatives and friends of those who have killed themselves, past and present suicide attempters, those with a history of depression, and those whose social support is weak because of things like a troubled family, a divorce, or a recent move.

Similar to suicides following the deaths of rock and movie idols, one teenage suicide following another may be caused partly by identification with the dead young person—and compounded by the teenager's own troubles. In a way, then, a teenage suicide itself can be thought of as a "trigger factor." In some circumstances, it could serve as a spark for others. Part of that spark is that a troubled teen, feeling that there's no way out, can view another's suicide as an answer, a way to cope. Just as in the case of a parent's suicide, this role-modeling makes it "okay." Instead of seeking realistic solutions to problems, the young person turns to suicide as an acceptable problem-solver.

When a teenager is in the middle of a painful situation—a relationship that hurts or a school problem that's rough—it's not easy to sit back and calmly assess the reality that, tough as it all is, eventually the pain will lessen. The school problem will diminish in importance. Even a restrictive or unpleasant parental situation will eventually cease to be an all-important factor as the teenager gets older and leaves home.

Life and Death in the Movies

In the movie *Dead Poets Society*, problems with parents and self-esteem play major roles in a teenage suicide. Neil, a leader among his high-school classmates, appears supremely self-confident. But it's only a façade. His fatal weakness is that he doesn't have the courage to express to his father who he really is, to be himself. It's easier for Neil to try and please his father than to confront him. And he doesn't have the ability to realize that shortly, when he's eighteen, he'll be a lot freer. That this period in his life will pass. That it's not forever.

Neil goes to Mr. Keating, the English teacher, for advice because his father doesn't want him to perform in the school play:

> KEATING: *"Have you told your father what you just told me? About your passion for acting?"*
>
> NEIL: *"Are you kidding? He'd kill me."*
>
> KEATING: *"Then you're playing a part for him, too, aren't you? The part of the dutiful son.... You have to talk to your father and let him know who you really are....If that doesn't work, at least, by then, you'll be eighteen and able to do what you want."*
>
> NEIL: *"Eighteen? What about the play? The performance is tomorrow night."*
>
> KEATING: *"Then you'll have to talk to him before tomorrow night."*
>
> NEIL: *"Isn't there an easier way?"*
>
> KEATING: *"No. Not if you're going to stay true to yourself."*

Neil doesn't take Keating's advice. In the scene with his father after the play, he still can't get his feelings out. Even when his father says to tell him what he thinks, Neil says nothing. He doesn't think about what Keating said: that there's no "easy way" to be true to yourself, and that he'll soon be eighteen and able to do what he wants. Instead, all he can think to do is to shoot himself.

Tom Schulman, who wrote the screenplay for *Dead Poets Society*, says, "The reason Neil kills himself is because he is weak. When he says, 'Nothing,' to his father when his father asks him what his feelings are, he's no longer a hero. We wanted the message to be loud and clear that suicide is not a viable response to an overbearing parent."

The Media: Sensation or Education?

Some people feel that the news and entertainment media—newspapers, magazines, and especially television—play a part in the problem of youth suicide.

In watching the instant solutions prevalent in television situations, a troubled teen, especially one with problems similar to those shown on the screen, can get a badly distorted idea of what's really needed to work things out. In real life, with no script that has to finish in an hour, problems take a lot of patience and hard work to solve.

And, most importantly, they take time. No one gets over breaking up with someone in an hour or after one quick chat with Mom or a teacher. No one feels okay in a half hour about not making the sports team. It takes a lot more time and a lot more talking than what one sees on TV.

The other problem with television, and this also goes for magazines and movies, is that so many of the teens and adults who are featured look and seem so perfect. Teenagers who have insecurities—and who doesn't?—about their self-image and their looks compare themselves to those "perfect people." They feel those glossy photo or screen faces and bodies are what they themselves are supposed to be. And, if they don't match whatever the ideal is for that season, there must be something wrong with them.

The media have also been accused of exacerbating the problem and effects of teenage suicide by publicizing and often sensationalizing the facts. The hard-hitting language of TV newscasts and the glaring headlines and bombardment of articles that focus on the shocking details of the suicide keep the tragedy in the forefront, without an educational component to help people deal with it. Then there's the language used in some news publications: for example, in articles about the Omaha suicides: "four other...students tried to kill themselves...but failed." And again: "Five attempted ...and three...succeeded." Unfortunately, the choice of words can be interpreted to mean that it is "successful" to cop out of life by committing suicide, and that one is a "failure" if one does not die from an attempt.

According to Abraham Matus, "The media contributes to teenage suicides an awful lot. It's like copycat murders. You know [that] when you read about it in the newspapers, a week later another person's going to do it."

However, Judie Smith, of Dallas, maintains that "someone doesn't become suicidal just by picking up a newspaper and seeing that someone else has done it."

The media can help, too. Since newspapers, magazines, and especially TV are seen by so many young people, they can serve as educational tools to promote awareness of the problem of youth suicide. They can broadcast and publish hotline and crisis phone numbers. And they can contribute to opening up dialogues.

Opening up dialogues—talking about the problem—is the most effective weapon against teenage suicide. Ms. Smith, Mr. Matus, and nearly all other experts agree that the biggest danger is the prevention of discussion of the subject. This gives it more mystique, promotes more misinformation, and, ultimately, may cause more suicides. The proper kind of discussion—educational, informative, factual—is the chief defense we have against youth suicide. Sometimes the media can turn around and provide that educational and informative forum.

Mr. Matus says that a book like *Ordinary People*, by Judith Guest, can give people insight into teenage suicide. Individuals can try to understand what the young man was going through. Parents can see what they should or shouldn't do.

Ordinary People deals with the aftermath of a teenage suicide attempt. Seventeen-year-old Conrad is home after hospitalization, shakily trying to put his life back together. His upper-middle-class parents appear on the surface to be the perfect American family. They have high expectations for their son, which he has internalized. Nobody in the house talks about his or her real feelings. Everything is very nice and polite and smoothed over. However, the family is slowly unraveling. Each member—mother, father, son—has shut his own set of painful emotions inside and cannot share them.

A year or so before Conrad's suicide attempt, he and his older brother, Buck, were in a boating accident. Conrad held onto his end of the capsized boat, but his brother couldn't hang on and drowned.

No one in the family talks about the accident. Conrad is full of "survivor guilt," a term referring to the feeling of guilt over being alive after another person dies. He feels that his parents, especially his mother, blame him for not being able to save his brother. He feels that his parents wish he had been the one who died, since his brother seemed to be the favored child.

And, just as in real families, Conrad's parents missed the signals. When his father thinks back to the time before the suicide attempt, he remembers that the school principal had called to tell him that Conrad's grades were falling. At that point, his father recalls, he felt that "something was terribly wrong." And immediately before the suicide attempt, Conrad's worried grandfather had phoned his son-in-law, saying that something was wrong with Conrad.

In his therapy sessions, Conrad begins to unlock some of his pent-up guilt feelings that caused his suicide attempt, together with his unrealistic expectations of himself. His therapist suggests that maybe Conrad is carrying too heavy a load and trying to take on too many things at once. Because he missed nearly a year of school while he was in the hospital, he's taking a demanding course load. He is also putting in many hours every day practicing for the very competitive swim team.

Conrad initially rejects Dr. Berger's advice to slow down. Then he finds out that one of his friends from the hospital killed herself. With his own suicidal feelings erupting again, he calls his therapist for help.

This is the turning point in Conrad's healing process. Finally realizing he wasn't guilty of causing his brother's death, that nobody, in fact, was guilty, and that he doesn't have to be perfect, Conrad can have a life of his own. He can be himself. He can live.

A television drama dealing with teenage suicide used as its fictional heroine Nadia Comaneci, the Romanian gymnast who became an Olympic star at age fourteen.

In the TV film *Nadia*, she is depicted as having been in training constantly, day in and day out, from the age of six. Competing and winning are all-important—and perfection is expected. At the 1976 Montreal Olympics, she stuns everyone with her flawless performances and wins three gold medals. Nadia scores the first perfect 10 in a gymnastic Olympic event. Her friends and teammates soon become jealous of the attention she's getting.

Because of a disagreement between her coach and the government sports authorities, Nadia and her teammates are whisked off to a faraway city. She isn't even able to say goodbye to the coach who's been part of her life for so long. In her new environment, without her strict trainer, she begins to gain weight. At about the same time, Nadia's mother tells her that she and Nadia's father are getting a divorce.

Nadia is shown suffering two losses, one right after the other. The two men in her life who were most important to her, her father and her coach, have been taken away from her. She's in strange surroundings, bewildered by her fame, her friends' alienation, and her adolescence. She's lost her conditioning. Now she can't live up to her expectations of herself. In addition, she thinks the boy she's been dating is no longer interested in her.

Feeling despondent, rejected, and totally hopeless, Nadia picks up a cup of laundry bleach and drinks it.

In this fictional portrayal of Nadia Comaneci, many of the elements that may lead to a suicide attempt are present: her drive for perfection and the sudden changes in her life—fame, a move, adolescence, alienation of her friends, loss of her beloved coach, and her parents' divorce. The "trigger factor" was another feeling of loss—of her boyfriend to another girl.

Whether Nadia Comaneci ever tried to kill herself in real life is uncertain. What we're concerned with here is the portrayal of a suicidal syndrome.

Another television program, "The Facts of Life," devoted an episode to teenage suicide. This segment, called "The

Breaking Point," was described by Kim Fields, a star of the program, who was then fourteen:

An ambassador's daughter comes to the boarding school as a new student. She's moved around from country to country all her life and has never had a chance to make friends. She is just beginning to make friends with Tootie, the character played by Kim Fields, when she finds out her parents are getting a divorce. She overdoses on pills and dies in the hospital.

Tootie is the one who finds her unconscious.

"And that was really rough," said Kim. "Because I was the youngest on the show. And I was her friend on the show. She was supposed to be like my older sister.

"Tootie reacted," continued Kim, "by just freaking out. The ambulance took her to the hospital. And then we got the news that the girl had passed away. It was a real hard episode.

"They showed us packing up her things. And we kept asking ourselves, 'Why would she do something like that?' Tootie," added Kim, "was really angry that her friend didn't talk to her about what was going on in her life."

Kim said that everyone on the show felt the subject was handled well. Even more important was a letter the cast got from a teenage girl. The girl wrote that she'd felt she couldn't go on. She couldn't talk to her friends. And she'd planned to commit suicide with an overdose of pills.

"But two nights before, she saw the show—and she didn't do it," reported Kim. "Somehow, watching the show made her think twice about suicide as a solution to her problems. To know that you saved a life through a TV show is a wonderful feeling."

CHAPTER SIX

Prevention

Kim Fields herself has had real-life pressures that have made her think of suicide at times.

One of these is her weight.

"No joke, I've thought of suicide," she said. "Television makes you look much heavier. That can be real nerve-wracking. When you're trying to lose weight, it can be real hard. And when there's a lot of people who look up to you, it can all be a little much. I just break down and cry sometimes."

Identity crises, which plague young people who are not in the limelight, are a double-whammy for those in Kim's business.

"You work with adults a lot, so you're treated like one," she explained.

Talking About It Helps

What has helped Kim deal with her troubled feelings is being able to talk about them to her mother and her friends. But she admitted that it wasn't easy for her to discuss her problems or ask for help. It's always been easier for her to help others. Like Kim, many young people care about others and want to help them.

Because of this, teaching teenagers to help each other is now one of the most commonly used approaches to youth suicide prevention. In community after community, high-schoolers are being trained to help save one another's lives. Educators and mental health professionals have realized that often teenagers will talk first—and sometimes only—to other teenagers about problems. Put that together with the fact that most young people really care about each other and are eager to help—and you have a powerful force against youth suicide.

Peer counseling and peer leadership groups are now in place in many schools in all parts of the country. The idea behind the groups is that teenagers who are trained in listening to classmates and aware of the danger signs will be the first line of defense in a crisis and will immediately alert an adult professional to the situation.

With that premise in mind, Glen Rock High School in suburban New Jersey formed a peer counseling group. It got started because a lot of students were coming to school administrators about their problems. And the administrators began to wonder, "What happens to the ones who are afraid to come to an adult to talk?"

Juniors and seniors were approached to begin a peer counseling group. The criterion: to be an open, caring, supportive good listener. Members of the community's service agencies were asked to be resource people.

Fifteen high school juniors and seniors make up the group each year. Most of the students in this middle-to-upper-class small suburban school know who the peer counselors are.

"Mainly, people know us by word of mouth," says Julie, sixteen. "And if people know someone has a problem, they'll tell them to come and talk to me."

Another peer counselor, eighteen-year-old Frank, remarks, "You see a lot of depression coming from things like achievement and college choices. There are expectations from all kinds of people—teachers, friends—not just parents. A whole lot of things will get piled up. They'll take on too much, like the drama club, the school paper, and they have to decide what college they want to go to, what they want to do for the rest of their life. And everything comes down at once. They feel they have no way out, they get really depressed."

Setting Priorities

What does Frank do when someone feels this way?

"I just sit down and say, 'Look at it, see what your priorities are, see how important these things are to you. If some of them aren't so important, don't worry about them.' Then," he says, "they start to calm down. If you can get past that big moment of panic, you can start thinking about what's going on."

Colleges, career choices, and grades are high on the pressure list the peer counselors help fellow students with.

Alicia, seventeen, comments, "I've talked to a lot of people about achievement and college. Their parents are pressuring them to do different things about college. And they're not achieving as they want to achieve. So they feel really depressed. Mostly," she says, "I listen. I give options. One guy's parents were pressuring him into choosing a career for his whole life—and he was only seventeen. It was like, 'If you don't decide tomorrow, you're not going to college.' He had a big problem."

What Alicia suggested to him was to try to sit down with his parents and tell them how confused he was feeling. If that didn't work, she said, maybe a family talk with a professional counselor would help.

As in many suburban middle-class communities, grades and the college one goes to are considered very important.

Although grades, college, and career choices are stressful, especially for high school seniors, there are also the other problems teens everywhere face: divorce of parents, popularity, boyfriend/girlfriend problems, peer pressure, and sexual identity.

Teenagers have come to Glen Rock's peer counselors thinking they might be homosexual. They can't tell anybody. They feel as if this is the worst thing that could ever have happened to them. They're saying, "I'm not sure if I am." But they find themselves, for example, looking at other guys instead of girls. And they just don't know. One person who talked about suicide said, "I've thought about it before. And if I don't resolve the homosexuality question, I'm going to do it." Ultimately, he was persuaded by school administrators to talk to his parents, and he's now in counseling.

Seventeen-year-old Greg says, "I talked to a girl at a weekend retreat who told me she contemplated suicide twice. 'Why?' I asked her. She said, 'My parents got a divorce; I thought it was my fault.' She talked about her parents' fighting, how her father hit her mother, how she'd just sit up in her room and cry." Greg recalls, "The next week, I went back to check up on her. She was coping better. She'd needed people to talk to."

Beth, seventeen, comments, "One person whose parents were divorced when she was six wound up growing up on her own with her sister. Her mother had to work. That affects you when you're growing up if you don't get it worked out. It gave her other problems—she felt her boyfriend meant everything to her. When they had a fight, she felt she couldn't live without him."

Frank remarks, "Some kids' parents really belittle kids' problems and say, 'Come on, your problems can't be that big. We're going out and earning money. What kind of problems can you have?' They really don't see how big a thing it is in a small town to lose two friends. The other ten who like the two you lose aren't going to be your friends anymore. Parents don't see it's a major thing in your life. They say, 'Big deal. You're not going to commit suicide.' So you need someone around who realizes that if you're talking about it, you're pretty serious and you might mean it."

Secrets Never to Keep

What do peer counselors do if someone tells them he's thinking of killing himself?

Greg says, "If that person says they're going to commit suicide, you have to turn them over to a responsible adult. You don't want to mess with anyone's life."

Frank adds, "Even if they hate me for it, I'd rather have them hate me forever than find them dead the next day."

Next door, in Ridgewood, New Jersey, school psychologist Abraham Matus set up a peer counseling group in 1979 after two teenage suicides had shocked the community.

Ridgewood is another suburb with high achievement standards for its young people.

Mr. Matus, like the administrators in Glen Rock, trains his peer counselors in listening, being nonjudgmental, and, most importantly, in not keeping secrets when it comes to saving lives.

"You throw confidentiality out the window if there's something self-destructive. And I've never had a person who's left me because of that. I invariably hear a sigh of relief after I say that I will do whatever is necessary to take measures to save their life, to protect them, to contact people who are responsible," he states.

Mr. Matus firmly believes that the rise in teen suicides can be stopped.

"It's not magic. You can prevent suicide. It's a matter of understanding. A lot of kids' lives could be saved if people in the schools were aware of what's going on. What we need to do is to have classes set aside to teach this phenomenon to kids."

His reasoning is that because they are with teenagers five days a week, six hours a day, teachers and other school personnel are in a better position than anyone else to spot behavior changes and trouble signs in young people. All they need, he says, is proper training and awareness regarding teenage suicide.

Education and awareness were the initial responses in Cherry Creek, a suburb of Denver, after four teen suicides in 1980 and 1981. The school system, in conjunction with mental health professionals, developed crisis team training. There are now eight crisis teams in the Cherry Creek middle and high schools. The teams consist of administrators, teachers, and guidance counselors.

Says Dr. Bill Porter, director of mental health for the Cherry Creek schools, "The responsibility of the crisis team is to know the available community resources, to be able to connect kids—and their parents—with them. We found that education alone wasn't enough. The biggest problem is that people don't know how to access resources. Our role is to be connectors, not intervenors. We needed to develop a continuum, connecting the kid with the appropriate resource person.

"For example, someone from a school's crisis team who spots a kid who looks troubled might say, 'Hey, it looks like you're having a rough day. I know somebody who can help us.' The team person walks the kid to the guidance counselor's office, and the counselor connects him with a community agency."

Barbara Blanton, executive director of the Crisis Center of Collin County, Texas, which began operating during the cluster of youth suicides, talks about the partnership of the schools and the community in suicide awareness and prevention.

"The community accepted the fact that it was not just a school problem, not just a family problem, but a community problem—and that everyone needed to work on it."

The Crisis Center works with teachers for suicide prevention for all students in grades nine through twelve. Volunteers and staff at the Crisis Center teach approximately 7,000 young people a year about suicide prevention.

"We teach kids how to help a friend: to encourage the friend to talk and then to go to an adult they trust, so that we can put a safety net under that youngster," said Ms. Blanton.

"And," she added, "we know that many of the clusters started not with a suicide but with an accidental or traumatic death. So we put a system into place to mobilize if and when there's a violent death of a young person. For instance, if a teenager is killed in a car accident, police call the school and the Crisis Center. Center personnel and school counselors work with the kids identified as 'high risk'—siblings, friends, classmates, those having problems of their own.

"It's a lot like a delayed reaction to a plane crash. After the trauma, kids are crashing and burning. They need a safe place to go and talk about their feelings."

Everyone now seems to agree that "high-risk" teenagers are not just siblings or good friends of the suicide, but also classmates and those with problems. In addition, experts say, it's not just a suicidal death but any traumatic death that could serve as a "trigger factor." Prevention strategies are now being tailored to include a broader range of people and incidents that need monitoring and intervention.

Many school systems have brought suicide prevention and awareness to students in one form or another, usually in conjunction with community resource agencies. Not every school system, however, favors this type of preventive teaching. In some areas of the country, the old taboos are alive and well. One of these school systems is in a northern New York City suburban area that was plagued by a cluster of teen suicides. In an article in the *New York Times*, a teacher wrote that after the suicide of a former student, he'd read poetry about suicide and discussed it in class. A parent complained, and the principal of the school subsequently banned any discussion of the subject.

In the article, the teacher wrote, "I have not learned if it is harmful to discuss suicide in class or to read literature that deals with it. Among the misconceptions that people are said to have about suicide is the belief that if you ask a person about suicide you will be planting a seed in his mind and the person will do it."

Even school systems that teach suicide prevention and awareness have usually had to struggle to get acceptance and approval for the programs. It's not a subject that parents, teachers, administrators, and school board members can deal with easily or comfortably.

According to Charlotte Ross, a suicide expert who's worked with the northern California school system, "There's a notion of contagion that if kids hear about suicide, it'll get them to do it. What happens then is an attempt to repress information, which makes them that much more curious. They'll try to talk about it and people won't talk to them.

"They won't tell a teacher because of fear the teacher might tell the parents or the principal. Then they might get kicked out of school or locked up in a hospital. Suicide still means 'you're crazy.' So the person they tell is usually another kid. But kids have a lot of misinformation. They don't have the facts. And there's still a conspiracy of silence surrounding suicide. The teenager's Eleventh Commandment is: 'Thou shalt not fink on a friend.'"

Because kids were going to other kids anyway, Ms. Ross decided they needed more information about how to help each other, and she began to work with the schools. One of her first projects was called "Share a Secret, Save a Friend," which dealt with the lethal consequences of not telling.

In 1981 the California State Senate, worried about teen suicides in the state, held hearings in its Select Committee on Children and Youth. The results were a state-mandated program for youth suicide prevention in the schools. The California State Office of Education asked Charlotte Ross and Dr. Michael Peck, a suicide expert in the Los Angeles area, to develop the program for California schools.

Call for Help

Many of the school programs, like the ones in California, work with community crisis centers and help lines. Help lines, hotlines, and crisis lines use the telephone as a way for a troubled young person to get help. The telephone talk, especially since it's anonymous, is often the first step in reaching out and getting help. The young person may then feel comfortable enough to make an appointment with one of the counseling agencies the help-line worker might suggest. If nothing else, the help line can get the troubled teenager through a crisis—just by being there for him.

A major prevention program that uses the call-for-help approach is an international suicide intervention group called The Samaritans. It was founded in 1958 in London by an Episcopal minister, because of a teenage suicide.

The minister was Chad Varah. One of the members of his congregation was a thirteen-year-old girl who was menstruating for the first time and didn't know what was happening. No one had ever explained the facts of life to her. She was having a sexual relationship and thought the menstruation was a punishment for her sins, possibly a venereal disease. She killed herself.

After her death, Mr. Varah realized that a good number of suicides could be prevented by providing people with information and help. He then organized The Samaritans for this purpose. Its name is believed to originate from the biblical "Good Samaritan," who helped people in distress. The Samaritans' purpose is to "befriend the suicidal, lonely, and despairing."

There are now two hundred branches in thirty-three countries all over the world. Since the first branch opened, England, which has the largest number of Samaritans centers, is reported to have had a 38-percent decrease in suicides.

The first American branch opened in Boston in 1974. Since then, branches have organized in Lawrence, Framingham, Fall River, and Falmouth, Massachusetts; Keene and Manchester, New Hampshire; Providence, Rhode Island; Hartford, Connecticut; Washington, D.C.; and Albany and New York City, New York.

All the Samaritans groups have hotlines and most are

available twenty-four-hours-a-day. They are staffed by volunteers and are not church-related, although the offices may be housed in a church. All callers remain anonymous and information is kept confidential.

A help-line worker at the New York City Samaritans described a dialogue he had with a sixteen-year-old suicidal teenager who called for help:

> *SAMARITAN: Can I help you?*
> *GIRL: Yes. I'm looking for a place to stay. I'm homeless.*
> *SAMARITAN: Where are you? Are you here in the city?*
> *GIRL: Yes, I'm in the city.*
> *SAMARITAN: Have you been here long?*
> *GIRL: About a week.*
> *SAMARITAN: Where have you been staying?*
> *GIRL: I've been staying at a women's shelter one night and in different buildings. I went home with a guy one night. I don't want to do that again.*
> *SAMARITAN: Where do you come from? Do you have a family out there? (She was from the Midwest.) Do they care about you? Do you feel cared for?*
> *GIRL: No, they don't. No, no, they don't. My mother's too busy with her boyfriend. Her new boyfriend.*
> *SAMARITAN: Did that precipitate the running away?*
> *GIRL: Yes. Another "uncle" I couldn't stand. So I hitchhiked to New York. I don't want to be on the streets. I don't want to go back home. I don't see any future.*
> *SAMARITAN: Are things in your life so bad right now that you're considering suicide?*
> *GIRL: Yes.*
> *SAMARITAN: Do you have a plan in mind? Do you have the means available?*
> *GIRL: I could always jump or run in front of a car.*
> *SAMARITAN: Do you have a time set?*

GIRL: No, no. I'm not completely sold on the idea. It's not the first thing I'm going to do. But I'm not going to live this way.
SAMARITAN: I don't blame you. You sound like a nice young woman who deserves a chance. Things have really been bad to date. And I think perhaps you deserve a lot of credit, you have a lot of courage, to come through what you have. What else have you thought about doing?
GIRL: I've only been here a short period, but maybe I could live here. I don't want to go back there.

What The Samaritans try to do is to inject a recognition of the callers' power, rather than their powerlessness. This helps their self-esteem—to know that they can affect the direction of their lives. Often, they don't realize their own resources.

A seventeen-year-old New York City boy spoke to The Samaritans from a pay phone at the foot of the bridge from which he was about to jump.

He was feeling: "They'll be sorry when I'm dead. They'll all be at the funeral." He felt wronged. He had restrictive parents and he was very angry at them. He felt very isolated from his peers. His self-esteem was suffering because he felt he was being treated like a child. And he was under the influence of alcohol, which amplified his feelings.

What The Samaritan help-line worker said to him was, "You're going to be dead. You won't know who's at your funeral. You won't know if they came. And, do you realize, if your body isn't found for a couple of days and goes out to sea three or four times, they may not even recognize you. Or you may never be found. So the hard reality is that your body will bloat. It will not be very pretty. It's not going to be pleasant."

The Samaritans don't say, "It'll be better tomorrow." What they do say is, "You must really be in pain. You must be hurting."

The rise in teen suicides has prompted crisis and hotline services to reach out to teenagers in school and community programs. Concern for the nation's young people led the United States Congress to conduct an investigation into the issue. In 1983, the Select Committee on Children, Youth, and Families heard testimony from psychiatrists, psychologists, and crisis center directors.

The day-long hearings were entitled "Teenagers in Crisis: Issues and Programs." They were cochaired by Representative Lindy Boggs of Louisiana and Representative George Miller of California.

Representative Boggs reported, "Two things stand out as primary pressure points in teen suicides. First, young people who have been abused are more likely to be suicide victims. Second, in affluent neighborhoods, where both parents and siblings are achievers, the pressure to achieve is very, very strong to be accepted. Often," she said, "the ones who seem very involved in school with various activities and who seem to be 'no problem' are very troubled. And with a divorce, they frequently feel they're a terrible economic burden on the parent they're left with. In addition, children feel they were responsible for or helped cause the divorce. And they may feel abandoned by the other parent."

Communities Respond

To deal with the nation's teen suicide crisis, particularly the "cluster" or "contagion" phenomenon, the Centers for Disease Control (CDC) issued a number of recommendations to communities for prevention and containment of clusters:

Communities should develop their own response system before the onset of a suicide cluster. The system should involve all sectors of the community and the relevant community resources should be identified. The response plan should be implemented when a suicide cluster occurs in the community or when traumatic deaths occur, especially among teenagers or young adults. The first step in a community response should be to contact and prepare groups who will carry out the community plan. The response should avoid glorification and sensationalization of the suicides. Persons who may be at high risk should be identified and have at least one screening interview with a trained counselor; these persons should be referred for further counseling or other services as needed. Elements in the environment that might increase suicides should be identified and changed, and long-term issues suggested by the nature of the cluster should be addressed.

This is exactly what one of the "cluster" communities did. Immediately after the suicides, the town of Bergenfield, New Jersey, developed a Community Response Team, headed by Reverend Stephen Giordano. The team consists of clergy, school personnel, mental health professionals, and members of school and town administration. The team instituted a twenty-four-hour crisis hotline, which has since become a country-wide operation. It opened a teen drop-in center and hired outreach workers to serve as a bridge to potentially troubled teens. Dropouts were identified as high-risk young people (in this community, the cluster involved high school dropouts). The outreach workers made contact with teenagers who had dropped out of school during the past five years—over 100 young people—and referred them to job training or mental health programs.

"We want to help get their lives onto a positive track," says Reverend Giordano. "One of the main problems is that these kids don't know how to access all the services that are out there."

In the aftermath of the cluster suicides, Bryan High School in Omaha, Nebraska, has become a resource providing consultants to other high schools in the area.

Says Robert Whitehouse, Bryan High principal, "We help others head off possible suicides. We go to other schools and say, 'Look, these are the kinds of things that can happen, that did happen.' And we share some of the positive results of bringing the school back together again after the tragedy."

In Bothell, Washington, a suburb of Seattle, the Youth Suicide Prevention Center provides peer group counseling and support for teens who have problems. Counseling is done by teams of mental health professionals and teens are referred through their friends, schools, and the community's crisis phone line.

The youth center works as a community resource in the area's schools for suicide prevention and awareness.

"Of the four hundred teenagers we've counseled in the past four years, many of whom said they've attempted—none have committed suicide," said Brian Jung, resource development coordinator of the center. "That's the important thing. The need, the demand for help is there. And the kids are seeking help."

A national suicide prevention project, SAIL, was begun in 1987 by the Green County Council of Camp Fire in Tulsa, Oklahoma, after the suicide of a twelve-year-old boy who'd been a member of the council. After his death, a council worker found a small wooden sailboat he'd made in the group. The sailboat was chosen for an emblem and the name, SAIL, stands for Self-Acceptance Is Life.

Says Cathie Holland, director of the Green County Council, who began the program with her daughter, "We decided we had to do something to help save even one life, if we could."

At the National Camp Fire Organization Conference in

1988, the young people picked teen suicide for a discussion topic.

"They said, 'People won't talk about it,'" said Ms. Holland. "That's when we made the subject into a positive experience: that is, 'You'll be able to help a friend.'"

SAIL, which teaches suicide awareness and how to get help for oneself or a friend, now has branches in forty states and British Columbia.

Everyone's Problem, Everyone's Solution

Youth suicide is not a teenager's problem. It's not a family problem. It's not a school problem. It's a community problem—everyone's problem. A youth suicide affects the entire community. Young people are the future of a community, and, by extension, the larger community—the country. Young people must feel valued at home, in school, and by their community. To prevent youth suicide, the members of a community must work together.

Parents, schools, and communities have to face the reality that a suicidal teenager can be anyone's child—the young man or woman next door or right at home.

Divorce, moving, child abuse: these are stressful elements in a teenager's life. And today's extra pressures—achievement–oriented society, peer pressures—they're there, too. Teenagers need to learn how to cope with these and learn to say no to peer pressures they don't want or feel ready for. They need to learn to gauge themselves, to know and feel comfortable with what they can reasonably expect of themselves. They need to know that they don't have to be, and shouldn't try to be, perfect. They need to learn to accept themselves. And they need a "safe" place to talk and a person to express their feelings to.

Keep in mind that although stressful elements are a matter of course in many teenagers' lives, most young people are not suicidal. Most aren't depressed. And most are looking forward to a satisfying, happy life as an adult.

No one has all the answers about teenage suicide. One thing nearly everyone agrees on regarding prevention is that for young people to feel good about themselves, they must feel cared for. If they feel they matter to others, they can better cope with bad times and look forward to the future.

It's easier and more comfortable not to talk about the possibilities of teenage suicide. But mental health professionals and educators say that talking and teaching about suicide are the most effective weapons against it.

Time and again, when young people are at last confronted with their suicidal feelings in a supportive, nonjudgmental manner by their peers, teachers, and counselors, they respond in a positive way. In fact, they are usually relieved to finally get those feelings out. They are grateful for the caring and support from those around them.

Those who work with teenagers in crisis say that many potential suicides are headed off by simply allowing those feelings to be vented in a supportive, therapeutic environment. Even if the suicidal impulses remain, ventilation can be the first step toward unlocking those feelings that, if they stay bottled up, can kill.

Being a good friend and listener does not qualify a person to be a responsible therapist for a suicidal friend or classmate. However, a friend can be that first listener, that first step toward getting help. Whether in a one-to-one relationship or in a peer counseling group, teenagers will often turn to their friends or classmates before anyone else. Sometimes, another teen is the only one the suicidal person talks to.

It is a big responsibility when your friend or classmate tells you that he doesn't want to go on living, he's got nothing to live for, and he might as well be dead.

You listen, nod your head sympathetically, murmur understandingly. But then he says, "Swear you won't tell. This is our secret. Promise, or I won't be your friend anymore."

There is only one thing to do: tell. Tell a responsible adult immediately.

Tell a parent, a teacher, a guidance counselor, a clergyman, a mental health worker. As for your troubled friend's secret, what's more important—his secret or his life?

Where
to Go
for Help

To get immediate help for a suicide crisis, phone your local hospital emergency room. Or, if your town has a crisis center or hotline, phone there. Many community mental health centers also have hotlines or walk-in services.

Here is a list of large centers that specifically deal with suicide crises. They may be called by anyone, from any part of the country, day or night. They will help you or someone you know who needs help, or they will refer you to a help center in your location:

Suicide Prevention Center
1041 So. Menlo
Los Angeles, California 90006
213-386-5111

Suicide Prevention and Crisis Center of San Mateo County
1811 Trousdale Drive
Burlingame, California 94010
North county hotline: 415-692-6655, 6656, 6733, 6743
South county hotline: 415-368-6655, 6659
Coast hotline: 415-726-6655

Alachua County Crisis Center
730 N. Waldo Road, Suite 100
Gainesville, Florida 32601
904-376-4444

Baton Rouge Crisis Intervention Center, Inc.
2424 Bunker Hill
Baton Rouge, Louisiana 70808
Hotline: The Phone: 504-924-3900

Bergen County Suicide Hotline
Hackensack, New Jersey
201-262-HELP

Suicide Prevention Center, Inc.
Main P.O. Box 1393
Dayton, Ohio 45406
Hotline: 513-223-4777

Crisis Intervention Center
P.O. Box 40752
Nashville, Tennessee 37204
Hotline: 615-244-7444

Suicide and Crisis Center
2808 Swiss Avenue
Dallas, Texas 75209
Hotline: 214-828-1000

Crisis Intervention of Houston
P.O. Box 130866
Houston, Texas 77219
Hotline: 713-228-1505

Crisis Center of Collin County
Plano, Texas 75086
Hotline: 214-881-0088

Youth Suicide Prevention Center
P.O. Box 844
Bothell, Washington 98041
206-481-0560

CARE Crisis Line
Everett, Washington
Hotline: 206-258-4357
Toll-free hotline: 0-ZENITH-8770

Crisis Clinic of Seattle and King County
Seattle, Washington
Hotline: 206-461-3222
Toll-free hotline: 1-800-621-6040

The Samaritans:

Hartford, Connecticut
203-232-2121

Boston, Massachusetts
617-247-0220

Fall River, Massachusetts
508-536-6111

Falmouth, Massachusetts
508-548-8900

Framingham, Massachusetts
508-875-4500

Lawrence, Massachusetts
508-688-6607

Keene, New Hampshire
603-357-5505

Manchester, New Hampshire
603-644-2525

Albany, New York
518-463-2323

New York, New York
212-673-3000

Providence, Rhode Island
401-272-4044

Washington, D.C.
202-362-8100

Bibliography

Books

Alvarez, A. *The Savage God: A Study of Suicide.* NY: Random House, 1970.

Giovacchini, Peter, M.D. *The Urge To Die: Why Young People Commit Suicide.* NY: Macmillan Publishing Co., Inc., 1981.

Guest, Judith. *Ordinary People.* NY: The Viking Press, 1976.

Hendin, Herbert, M.D. *Suicide in America.* NY: W.W. Norton & Co., Inc., 1982.

Mack, John E., and Holly Hickler. *Vivienne: The Life and Suicide of an Adolescent Girl.* Boston: Little, Brown & Co., 1981.

McCoy, Kathleen. *Coping With Teenage Depression: A Parent's Guide.* NY: New American Library, Inc., 1982.

O'Neill, Cherry Boone. *Starving For Attention.* NY: The Continuum Publishing Co., 1982.

Roos, Stephen. *You'll Miss Me When I'm Gone.* NY: Delacorte Press, 1988.

Periodicals

"Another Teen Found Hanged," (AP), *The Star-Ledger,* February 16, 1984.

"Bergenfield's Tragic Foursome," *U.S. News & World Report,* March 23, 1987.

Blakeslee, Sandra. "Major Study Assesses the Children of Divorce," *The New York Times,* April 10, 1984.

Brooks, Andree. "Gauging Adolescents' Stress," *The New York Times,* November 29, 1983.

Brothers, Dr. Joyce. "Unrealistic American 'fairy tale' blamed for high teen suicide rate," *The Star-Ledger,* July 5, 1983.

"But for the Grace of God...," *U.S. News & World Report,* February 24, 1986.

"Campus Suicides on Rise," *Asbury Park Press,* September 1, 1983.

"CDC Recommendations for a Community Plan for the Prevention and Containment of Suicide Clusters," *Morbidity and Mortality Weekly Report,* Centers for Disease Control, Supplement, August 19, 1988, vol. 37, no. S–6.

"Cluster of Suicides and Suicide Attempts—New Jersey," *Morbidity and Mortality Weekly Report,* Centers for Disease Control, U.S. Dept. of Health and Human Services/ Public Health Service, April 15, 1988, vol. 37, no. 14.

Cole, Larry; Randazzo, John; and Carroll, Robert. "Another teenage suicide in W'chester," *Daily News,* March 16, 1984.

Colt, George Howe. "The enigma of suicide," *Harvard Magazine,* October 1983, vol. 86, no. 1.

"The Copycat Suicides," *Newsweek,* March 23, 1987.

"Could Suicide Be Contagious?," *Time,* February 24, 1986.

Curran, Barbara E., M.D. "Suicide," *Pediatric Clinics of North America,* November 1979, vol. 26, no. 4.

Davis, Robert. "Suicide Among Young Blacks: Trends and Perspectives," *Phylon*, September 1980.

Friedman, Stanford B., M.D., and Richard M. Sarles, M.D. "'Out of Control' Behavior in Adolescents," *Pediatric Clinics of North America*, February 1980, vol. 27, no. 1.

Gardner, Sandra. "Suicidal Behavior—A National Health Problem: How Can We Cope With It?" *Senior Scholastic Magazine*, January 9, 1981.

Green, Arthur H., M.D., "Child Abuse; Dimension of Psychological Trauma in Abused Children," *Journal of the American Academy of Child Psychiatry*, 22, 1983.

Hopkins, Barbara Winberg. "Running Away From It All: Suicide Among Troubled Youth," *Family Life Developments: Region II Resource Center on Children and Youth*, July-August 1983.

Iga, Mamoru, Ph.D. "Suicide of Japanese Youth," *Suicide and Life-Threatening Behavior*, Spring 1981, Volume II (1).

Jason, Kathrine. "Preschool Suicide," *OMNI*, September 1983.

Kraft, Scott. "6 suicides haunt Texas suburb," (AP) *The Sunday Record*, October 9, 1983.

Kranes, Marsha. "Teen Suicide In Church," *New York Post*, May 31, 1984.

Levin, Eric. "A Sweet Surface Hid A Troubled Soul In The Late Karen Carpenter, A Victim Of Anorexia Nervosa," *People Magazine*, February 21, 1983.

McGill, Douglas C., "Fordham Student Hangs Himself At Parents' Home in Westchester," *The New York Times*, February 26, 1984.

"Remembering Melissa," (editorial) *The New York Times*, March 30, 1983.

Rosenberg, Morris, and B. Claire McCullough. "Mattering: Inferred Significance and Mental Health Among Adolescents," *Research in Community and Mental Health*, 1981, vol. 2.

"Teenage Suicide: A Cry For Help," *Reform Judaism,* Winter 1983-84.

Wallerstein, Judith S., Ph.D. "Children After Divorce; Wounds That Don't Heal," *Perspectives in Psychiatric Care,* no. 3,4, 1987/88.

Weiss, Julian. "Trouble in paradise," *Psychology Today,* August 1984.

Williams, Lena. "2nd Teenage Suicide in Suburban Town," *The New York Times,* June 7, 1983.

————. "Suicide in New York's Suburbs: The Life and Death of Justin, 14," *The New York Times,* March 14, 1984.

"Youth's suicide 9th in a string," (AP) *The Record,* July 30, 1984.

Films and Television Dramas

Dead Poets Society, Touchstone Films, 1989.

Hirsh, Michael. *College Can Be Killing,* a production of WTTW/Chicago Public Television, 1978.

Nadia, a production of Tribune Entertainment Company, 1984.

Suggested Further Reading

Hughes, Dean. *Switching Tracks.* NY: Atheneum, 1982.
Hyde, Margaret and Elizabeth Held Forsyth. *Suicide: The Hidden Epidemic.* NY: Franklin Watts, 1978.
Klagsbrun, Francine. *Too Young To Die: Suicide and Youth.* Boston: Houghton Mifflin Co., 1976.
McKillip, Patricia A. *The Night Gift.* NY: Atheneum, 1976.
Roos, Stephen. *You'll Miss Me When I'm Gone.* NY: Delacorte Press, 1988.

Index

About
the
Authors

Sandra Gardner has been a regular freelance writer and weekly columnist for the New Jersey Weekly section of *The New York Times*, specializing in social issues involving youth and families. She is currently a staff writer for a large teaching hospital in New Jersey. This is the second edition of the third book Ms. Gardner has written for young adults. She lives with her family in Teaneck, New Jersey.

Gary B. Rosenberg graduated from Columbia University and the State University of New York-Downstate Medical Center College of Medicine. He is a board-certified adult and child psychiatrist. Dr. Rosenberg has written articles and lectured on teenage depression and suicide. He is presently Director, Adolescent Treatment Unit, Fair Oaks Hospital, in Summit, New Jersey.